STEVE JOBS

STEVE JOBS
THE MAN WHO THOUGHT
DIFFERENT

A BIOGRAPHY BY KAREN BLUMENTHAL

FEIWEL AND FRIENDS

NEW YORK

A Feiwel and Friends Book
An Imprint of Macmillan

Disclaimer: This biography is not endorsed by Apple.
This is an unauthorized/unofficial biography.

Library of Congress Cataloging-in-Publication Data Available

ISBN: 978-1-250-01557-0 (hardcover)
10 9 8 7 6 5 4 3 2 1

ISBN: 978-1-250-01445-0 (paperback)
10 9 8 7 6 5 4 3 2 1

Book design by Ashley Halsey

Feiwel and Friends logo designed by Filomena Tuosto

First Edition: 2012

macteenbooks.com

To Brad

Contents

Introduction

Three stories

On a warm June day in 2005, Steve Jobs went to his first college graduation—as the commencement speaker. The billionaire founder and leader of Apple Computer wasn't just another stuffed-shirt businessman. Though only fifty years old, the college dropout was a technology rock star, a living legend to millions of people around the world.

In his early twenties, Jobs almost single-handedly introduced the world to the first computer that could sit on your desk and actually do something all by itself. He revolutionized music and the ears of a generation with a spiffy little music player called the iPod and a wide selection of songs at the iTunes store. He funded and nurtured a company called Pixar that made the most amazing computer-animated movies—*Toy Story, Cars,* and *Finding Nemo*—bringing to life imaginary characters like never before.

Though he was neither an engineer nor a computer geek, he helped create one gotta-have-it product after another by always designing it with you and me, the actual users, in mind. Unknown to those listening to him that day, more insanely awesome technology was in the works, including the iPhone, which would put much of the power of a computer neatly into the palm of your hand. The father of four would be repeatedly compared with the inventor Thomas Edison and auto magnate Henry Ford, who both introduced affordable, life-changing conveniences that transformed the way Americans lived.

Yet for all his successes, Jobs also endured some very public failures. When he was thirty years old, he was summarily stripped of his duties at Apple for being too disruptive and difficult. He set out to build another computer company and missed the mark, blowing through millions of dollars of investors' money. He could be volatile, screaming at associates, competitors, and reporters. He sometimes cried when things didn't go his way and he regularly took credit for the ideas of others. He could be both charming and gratingly abrasive, sensitive and stunningly mean-spirited.

Some parts of his life sounded like a fairy tale right out of the movies: There was a promise made when he was a baby, romances, remarkable rebounds, and riches almost too big to be believed. Other parts were so messy and ugly, so very human, that they would never be considered family entertainment. He was both loved and hated, intensely admired and widely dismissed. People described him with the strongest words: Visionary. Showman. Artist. Tyrant. Genius. Jerk.

Wearing blue jeans and sandals under his graduation-day robe, Jobs stepped up to the microphone to speak in the same way he did just about everything: with intensity and passion. In a short speech to the twenty-three thousand students, parents, and friends gathered, he very publicly shared very personal insights into his own life.

"Today I want to tell you three stories from my life," he said.

No more. Just three stories that defined an amazing life and provided a guide designed for people at the beginning of their adult lives. To understand who Steve Jobs was and what he became, it helps to start there, with the first of those three stories.

Part 1

"The journey is the reward."

Steve Jobs (far left) hamming it up with school friends in the seventh grade.

1

Seeds

Steve Jobs's first story involved connecting dots, and it began with a most unusual promise.

Joanne Schieble was just twenty-three and attending graduate school in Wisconsin when she learned she was pregnant. Her father didn't approve of her relationship with a Syrian-born graduate student, and social customs in the 1950s frowned on a woman having a child outside of marriage. To avoid the glare, Schieble moved to San Francisco and was taken in by a doctor who took care of unwed mothers and helped arrange adoptions.

Originally, a lawyer and his wife agreed to adopt the new baby. But when the child was born on February 24, 1955, they changed their minds.

Clara and Paul Jobs, a modest San Francisco couple with some high school education, had been waiting for a baby.

When the call came in the middle of the night, they jumped at the chance to adopt the newborn, and they named him Steven Paul.

Schieble wanted her child to be adopted by college-educated parents. Before the adoption could be finalized, however, she learned that neither parent had a college degree. She balked and only agreed to complete the adoption a few months later, "when my parents promised that I would go to college," Jobs said.

Signing on to the hope of a bright future for their baby, the Jobs family settled in, adopting a daughter, Patty, a couple of years later. Little Steve proved to be a curious child, and a challenging one to rear. He put a bobby pin into an electrical outlet, winning a trip to the emergency room for a burned hand. He got into ant poison, requiring yet another trip to the hospital to have his stomach pumped. To keep Steve busy when he got up before the rest of the household, his parents bought him a rocking horse, a record player, and some Little Richard records. He was so difficult as a toddler, his mother once confided, that she wondered if she had made a mistake adopting him.

When Steve was five, his father, Paul, was transferred to Palo Alto, about forty-five minutes south of San Francisco. After serving in the Coast Guard during World War II, Paul had worked as a machinist and used-car salesman, and now was working for a finance company collecting bad debts. In his free time, he fixed up used cars and sold them for a profit, money that would go to Steve's future college fund.

The area south of San Francisco was largely undeveloped then and dotted with apricot and

Patty Jobs, freshman yearbook photo, 1972.

prune orchards. The family bought a house in Mountain View, and as Paul put together his workshop in the garage, he set aside a part of it, telling his son, "Steve, this is your workbench now." He taught Steve how to use a hammer and gave him a set of smaller tools. Over the years, Jobs remembered, his dad "spent a lot of time with me . . . teaching me how to build things, how to take things apart, put things back together."

His father's careful craftsmanship and commitment to the finest details made a deep impression. He "was a sort of genius with his hands. He can fix anything and make it work and take any mechanical thing apart and get it back together," Jobs told an interviewer in 1985. His father also stressed the importance of doing things right. For instance, his son learned, "When you're a carpenter making a beautiful chest of drawers, you're not going to use a piece of plywood on the back, even though it faces the wall and nobody will ever see it. You'll know it's there, so you're going to use a beautiful piece of wood on the back."

That was a lesson Jobs would apply over and over to new products from Apple. "For you to sleep well at night, the aesthetic, the quality, has to be carried all the way through," he said.

Clara supported her young son as well, babysitting the children of friends in the evenings to pay for swimming lessons. And because Steve was precocious and interested, she taught him to read, giving him a big head start at school.

Unfortunately for Steve, knowing how to read became something of a problem. Once in school, "I really just wanted to do two things," he remembered. "I wanted to read books because I loved reading books and I wanted to go outside and chase butterflies." What he didn't want to do was follow instructions. He bucked at the structure of the school day and soon was bored with being in class. He felt different from his classmates.

When he was six or seven years old, he told the girl across the street that he was adopted. "So does that mean your real parents didn't want you?" she asked.

The innocent question hit him like a punch to the stomach, planting a frightening thought that had never occurred to him. He ran into his house, sobbing. His parents quickly moved to comfort him and shoot down that notion. "They were very serious and looked me straight in the eye," he said. "They said, 'We specifically picked you out.'"

In fact, his parents thought he was very special—exceptionally bright, though also exceptionally strong-willed. Later, friends and colleagues would say that his drive and need for control grew out of a deep-rooted sense of abandonment. But he didn't see it that way. "Knowing I was adopted may have made me feel more independent, but I have never felt abandoned," he told a biographer. "I've always felt special. My parents made me feel special."

Some of his teachers, however, saw him more as a trouble-maker than as a special kid. Jobs found school so dull and dreadful that he and a buddy got their biggest kicks out of causing havoc. Many of the kids rode bikes to school, locking them up in racks outside Monta Loma Elementary School, and in third grade, Jobs and his friend traded the combination to their bike locks with many of their classmates. Then one day, they went out and switched the locks all around. "It took them until about ten o'clock that night to get all the bikes sorted out," he recalled.

The worst behavior was reserved for the teacher. Jobs and

his friend let a snake loose in the classroom and created a small explosion under her chair. "We gave her a nervous twitch," he said later.

He was sent home two or three times for his misbehavior, but he doesn't remember being punished for it. Instead, his father defended him, telling teachers, "If you can't keep him interested, it's your fault."

In fourth grade, he was rescued by a special teacher, Imogene "Teddy" Hill, who kindly showered attention on him during a particularly trying time at home. Impressed by a neighbor who seemed to be making a successful living selling real estate, Paul Jobs went to school at night and earned a real-estate license. But his timing was bad and the demand for housing slumped just as he was trying to break into the business.

One day, Mrs. Hill asked her students, "What is it that you don't understand about the universe?" Young Jobs answered: "I don't understand why all of a sudden my dad is so broke." Clara took a part-time job in the payroll department of a local company and the family took out a second loan on their house. For a year or so, money in the Jobs home was very tight.

Within a few weeks of having Jobs in her class, Mrs. Hill had sized up her unusual student. She offered Jobs a sweet bargain: If he could finish a math workbook on his own and get at least 80 percent right, she would give him five dollars and a giant lollipop.

"I looked at her like, 'Are you crazy, lady?' " Jobs said. But he took the challenge. Before long, his admiration and respect for Mrs. Hill were so great that he didn't need bribes anymore.

She returned the admiration, providing her precocious student with a kit for making a camera by grinding his own lens. But that didn't mean Jobs became an easy kid. Many years later, Mrs. Hill entertained some of Jobs's coworkers by showing them a photo of her class on Hawaiian Day. Jobs was in the middle, wearing a Hawaiian shirt. But the photo didn't tell the whole story: Jobs hadn't actually worn a Hawaiian shirt that day—but he had managed to convince a classmate to give him the shirt off his back.

Calling the teacher "one of the saints in my life," Jobs said, "I learned more that year than I think I learned in any year in school." And he credits her with moving him onto the right path. "I'm one hundred percent sure that if it hadn't been for Mrs. Hill in fourth grade and a few others, I would absolutely have ended up in jail," he said later.

With his interest in school reignited and his performance seemingly on track, Jobs was tested and scored so high that school officials recommended he skip a couple of grades. His parents agreed to let him skip just one.

Middle school was tougher academically and he still

wanted to chase butterflies. A sixth-grade report called him "an excellent reader," but noted "he has great difficulty motivating himself or seeing the purpose of studying reading." He was also "a discipline problem at times."

Seventh grade brought a much rougher crowd of classmates. Fights were common. Some students bullied the wiry kid who was a year younger than everyone else. Jobs was miserable, and in the middle of that year, he gave his parents an ultimatum: He said "if he had to go back to school there again, he just wouldn't go," his father recalled. They took him seriously. "So we decided we better move," his dad said.

His parents pulled together what little they had and bought a three-bedroom home in Los Altos, where the schools were top-notch—and safe. There, presumably, their gifted son might focus on his studies. But in the mid-1960s, times were changing. Jobs would soon have other things on his mind.

"For the times
they are
a-changin'."

—*Bob Dylan*

2

Woz

The new school was indeed an improvement, and Jobs found other boys who shared his interests. There, he would form friendships that eventually would change his life.

He was also lucky to be growing up in the Santa Clara Valley, a place chock-full of engineers and tinkerers who would help feed his growing passion for the expanding field of electronics.

Realizing his son didn't share his interest in cars and other kinds of mechanics, Paul Jobs had brought him electronic gizmos to take apart and study from the time he was in grade school. Steve Jobs also found a mentor in his old neighborhood, a Hewlett-Packard Company engineer named Larry Lang, who intrigued Jobs with an old-fashioned carbon microphone set up in his driveway that didn't need an electronic amplifier. Lang introduced the boy to Heathkits, a conglomeration of electronic parts and detailed instructions that let hobbyists build radios and other gadgets.

"You actually paid more money for them than if you just went and bought the finished product," Jobs remembered. But he was intrigued by how putting together the kits helped him understand how things worked and gave him confidence in what he could build. "These things were not mysteries anymore. I mean you looked at a television set (and) you would think that 'I haven't built one of those but I could. There's one of those in the Heathkit catalog and I've built two other Heathkits so I could build that,'" Jobs said. "It gave a tremendous level of self-confidence that, through exploration and learning, one could understand seemingly very complex things in one's environment."

Even after the family moved, Jobs stayed in touch with Lang, who helped get him involved in a Hewlett-Packard Explorers Club. Jobs and other students gathered on Tuesday nights in the company's cafeteria to hear engineers talk about their work. It was during one of those visits that Jobs saw a desktop computer for the first time. Computers in the 1960s ranged from refrigerator- to room-sized, usually requiring extra air-conditioning to keep from overheating. Hewlett-Packard had developed the 9100A, its first desktop scientific calculator, in 1968, advertising it as a "personal computer" that was "ten times faster than most machines at solving science and engineering problems."

"It was huge, maybe forty pounds, but it was a beauty of a thing," Jobs said. "I fell in love with it."

While trying to build his own frequency counter, which measures the pulses in an electronic signal, Jobs found himself short of parts. Without thinking twice about it, he looked up H-P founder, Bill Hewlett, in the phone book and called him at home. Hewlett graciously took the call and visited with Jobs for twenty minutes. By the time the chat ended, Jobs had gotten the parts as well as a contact for a summer job. He spent a summer on the manufacturing line, putting screws in frequency counters, which were used in laboratories and factories. "I was in heaven," he remembered.

People like Bill Hewlett helped make the Santa Clara Valley a magnet for engineers and technical specialists. In addition to the growing Hewlett-Packard operation in Palo Alto, the missile division of Lockheed Corporation in Sunnyvale, a nearby NASA research center, and Fairchild Semiconductor in San Jose offered an increasing number of jobs for the technically inclined. In addition, Stanford University in nearby Palo Alto and the University of California–Berkeley, a bit to the north, were hotbeds of science and technology.

The years of Jobs's childhood were a time of rapid innovation in the world of electronics, the science and technology of controlling the unseen flow of electricity to make things work. In the late 1940s, three scientists working at AT&T's Bell Labs—John Bardeen, Walter Brattain, and William

Shockley—invented the transistor, a tiny device that could direct and amplify electrons. The transistor was built around a material called a "semiconductor," neither a true insulator nor a conductor, which could send electric currents in one direction, but not the other. In time, silicon would become the preferred semiconducting material, and the tiny devices that resulted would become known as semiconductors or "chips."

In replacing bulkier, less reliable vacuum tubes, the transistor became the basis for all electronic devices, allowing scientists and engineers to make ever-smaller gadgets, like transistor radios that fit in a pocket, televisions that could sit on a shelf, calculators that fit in one's hand, and eventually a computer that could sit on a desk.

As Hewlett-Packard and the other companies grew and moved into making new kinds of equipment, semiconductors, and gadgets with increasing abilities, ambitious men left to start their own companies to come up with more innovations. It was, Jobs said later, "like those flowers or weeds that scatter seeds in hundreds of directions when you blow on them."

With so much activity and focus on chips and circuits, more and more people moved into the area. Orchards were bulldozed for new housing developments, and San Jose's population doubled in size between 1960 and 1970, while nearby Cupertino's quadrupled. The area would soon become known as Silicon Valley.

By the time Jobs was in junior high, his father was

working for a company that made lasers for electronics and medical products. Jobs developed an interest in that as well, building his own with spare parts he scrounged up or that his dad brought home, sometimes sharing his projects at junior high school.

A classmate, Bill Fernandez, became a good friend, working with Jobs on a science fair project and sharing other interests. Over the years, they would take long walks in the evening, talking about all sorts of serious matters, from the Vietnam War to girls, from drugs to religion. (In fact, throughout his life, Jobs would wrestle with big ideas and difficult matters by talking through them on long walks.)

At thirteen, Jobs had stopped going to the Lutheran church after confronting the church pastor with a magazine story about children starving in Africa. "Does God know about this and what's going to happen to those children?" he asked the pastor. When the pastor acknowledged that "yes, God knows about that," Jobs decided that he couldn't worship such a God.

Even so, he and Fernandez spent hours discussing spiritual matters. "We were both interested in the spiritual side of things, the big questions: Who are we? What is it all about? What does it mean?" Fernandez said. "Mostly it was Steve who would do the talking. . . . He would have a grand passion of the day, or something that was on his mind, and he would bend my ear for hours as we walked."

The year Jobs entered high school, 1968, was one of most tumultuous in modern American history. Reverend Martin Luther King, Jr., who had fought racial discrimination with nonviolent means, was assassinated in April. Robert Kennedy, a candidate for president, was shot and killed after a campaign speech a couple of months later. Opposition to the Vietnam War reached a fever pitch, with antiwar demonstrators rioting at the Democratic National Convention in Chicago.

Meanwhile, there was a curious new social phenomenon. In a 1967 cover story titled "The Hippies," *Time* magazine described the mostly white, middle-class, and well-educated young people who were "dropping out," rejecting college and traditional job paths in favor of seeking love, peace, and enlightenment—partly by experimenting with hallucinogenic drugs like marijuana and LSD. Getting their nickname from the 1950s beatnik term "hip" or "hipster," these hippies dressed in wildly colorful clothes, listened to "acid rock" like Jefferson Airplane and the Grateful Dead, and wore their hair long. The epicenter of the movement was the Haight-Ashbury neighborhood in nearby San Francisco.

By contrast, the Homestead High School that Jobs entered that year was still classic, sheltered suburbia. Made up of a series of one- and two-story buildings and surrounded by barbed wire, the campus looked something like a prison. The five hundred students in the class of 1972 were almost entirely white, with just two black students and a handful of Asian classmates. A strict dress code required boys' hair to be trimmed above the ear. Blue jeans were forbidden, so boys wore slacks and girls wore dresses and skirts, which had to be within three inches of their knees.

To classmates, Jobs could be cold and brittle and came off as extremely confident—maybe overly so. But he was also considered brainy and a very good student. Carlton Ho, who was the band drum major and now is a civil engineering professor, recalls that he and Jobs frustrated a math teacher by spending their class time scanning through Edmund Scientific catalogs and discussing the choices.

During their junior year, Jobs's friend Bill Fernandez began to spend evenings and weekends helping his neighbor Steve Wozniak build a small computer in Wozniak's garage. Wozniak, who was almost five years older than Jobs and four years ahead of him in school, had been a star math, science, and electronics student at Homestead. Though his family couldn't really afford it, his parents had allowed him to spend a year at the University of Colorado in Boulder. But Wozniak, or Woz, as his friends called him, was more interested in experimenting with the possibilities of the big computers on campus and playing bridge late into the night. By the end of the year, his other grades suffered, and he returned home to attend a community college for a year to study computer science.

Steve Jobs, junior yearbook photo, 1971.

Then, unsure about whether he might be drafted into the military during the Vietnam War and in need of more funds for college, Wozniak took a year off from school and joined a company as a computer programmer. (At that point, young men were drafted when they were twenty years old according to the number assigned to your birthday in an annual lottery; ultimately Wozniak's birthday had a high lottery number, meaning he wasn't likely to be drafted at all.)

While Jobs and Fernandez were deeply interested in electronics, Wozniak was obsessed with it. For years, he had collected manuals that explained how minicomputers, a smaller version of mainframes, were made, and he studied their components and connections. For fun, he then tried to sketch out designs that would allow them to be built with fewer parts.

The computer Wozniak and Fernandez were building wasn't much to see. Composed of spare parts they scrounged up, it had only enough memory to hold 256 typed characters, or about a sentence. Wozniak could write small programs on punch cards that prompted the computer to beep every three seconds or perform a function by flashing lights attached to the front. There was no keyboard or screen, and too little memory to do even simple math. Still, it could run a program. They dubbed it the Cream Soda Computer because they consumed so many bottles of cream soda while building it. (The computer died an early death when a surge from the power supply caused the circuits to blow out in a plume of smoke.)

Fernandez realized his two friends both loved electronics and playing pranks, and that they should meet. So one day, Jobs rode his bike over. Wozniak was washing his car down the street. "Hey, Woz," Fernandez shouted. "Come over here and meet Steve."

Despite the age difference, the two hit it off from the start. Jobs admired that Wozniak knew more about electronics than he did, and felt like his maturity, and Woz's immaturity, just about matched. Wozniak appreciated that "Steve got it right away. And I liked him. He was kind of skinny and wiry and full of energy."

They began hanging out together. Wozniak introduced Jobs to the music and powerful lyrics of Bob Dylan and the two began hunting down bootleg tapes of Dylan concerts. Before long, they would even be partners in a most unusual— and illegal—business.

Steve Jobs, senior yearbook photo, 1972.

Steve Wozniak, senior yearbook photo, 1968.

3

Phreaks

The transition from sophomore year to junior year was an eventful one for Jobs.

The summer after tenth grade, he continued his school-year job as a stock clerk at a local store that carried a vast array of electronics parts, much like the auto-parts outlets his father had taken him to as a kid. There, he had developed a vast knowledge of electronics parts and prices, as well as learning the basic rules of business. Almost intuitively, he understood profits, the difference between what the store paid for goods and what it could sell them for; occasionally, he would purchase parts at a local flea market and sell them for a profit to the store owner, who would then resell them at an even higher price.

With his various earnings, Jobs was able to buy a car, a small and often unreliable red Fiat, which allowed him to explore and visit older friends at Stanford and Berkeley.

As the 1970s arrived, the Vietnam War started to slowly wind down and the hippie culture began to creep into the valley. Jobs, always testing boundaries, began to experiment. He grew his hair long. He began smoking marijuana. His father was angry and upset to discover the drugs in his son's car and tried to get his son to promise he wouldn't do it again. The younger Jobs refused. "That was the only real fight I ever got in with my dad," he said.

At the same time, his interests began to broaden beyond science, math, and electronics. "I discovered Shakespeare, Dylan Thomas, and all that classic stuff. I read *Moby-Dick* and went back as a junior, taking creative-writing classes," he said.

Homestead High relaxed its dress code and allowed blue jeans. With a friend, Jobs formed the Buck Fry club, an inappropriate twist on the principal's last name that nevertheless had a faculty sponsor. The small group organized concerts with student bands that played jazz, blues, and progressive rock. Drawing on Jobs's knowledge of lasers, the club members created elaborate laser shows to pulse dots with the music and cover the stage in a rainbow of colors.

Buck Fry was also known for small pranks, like painting a toilet seat gold and cementing it on a planter. Once, they invited the principal to join them for breakfast. The place turned out to be a special setting—on the roof above the cafeteria, where they had set up a table and chairs. They also managed to hoist a Volkswagen Beetle to the roof.

After school, Wozniak introduced Jobs to a pocket-sized "TV jammer" he built during his freshman year of college that fuzzed up a television's picture by interfering with the transmission. While his college dorm mates were watching television, Woz would turn the device on. Someone watching the television would get up to try to fiddle with the picture by twisting knobs on the set. Woz would mess with the hapless viewer, turning the jammer on and off when the person touched the set so that it appeared that the touch had made the difference. Sometimes, by turning the device off and on, Wozniak could contort an unknowing viewer into a pretzel. (The prank so impressed Jobs that more than thirty years later, when his presentation clicker stopped working during an iPhone introduction, he stopped for a minute to share the story of Woz's jammer and demonstrate how someone might end up with one leg in the air and arms twisted all around.)

At the end of Jobs's junior year, the two Steves and a Wozniak friend conspired to congratulate the graduating class with a special banner. Using a tie-dyed sheet, they drew a highly realistic hand displaying the universal sign of disapproval, and then added a cheery "Best Wishes." They signed it SWAB JOB, a mix of their initials and Jobs's name.

The three planned to install the banner on the roof of

one of the buildings and unfurl it as the graduates walked by. But they had trouble getting the sheet to unroll properly. They spent several nights working on it. But the day of graduation, Wozniak got a call from Jobs. Someone else had pulled the sign down, and Jobs had gotten caught.

Only later did Wozniak learn that Jobs had bragged about the stunt to some friends, one of whom spoiled it.

In the fall of 1971, Wozniak returned to college, this time at Berkeley, about an hour north of Los Altos. He hadn't even started classes when his mom alerted him to an unusual article in *Esquire*: a group of pre-computer hackers was building little devices they called "blue boxes," which emitted the same sounds that the phone company used to transmit calls. Copying the tones to the exact frequency allowed users to capture phone lines and make calls for free anywhere in the world. They called themselves "phone phreaks."

Outsmarting the telephone company captivated Wozniak. Individuals had only recently been able to dial overseas calls themselves without going through an operator. Decades before cell phones, customers had only one phone company to choose from. And long distance was expensive: A three-minute, coast-to-coast call on the weekends cost 70¢, equivalent to almost $4 today. Calling during the week cost even more. The potential was startling.

Enthralled, Wozniak called his friend Steve Jobs and

started reading the article to him. That same day, the pair headed to the library to research the subject, discovering the exact frequencies in technical documents. Over several months, Wozniak worked on designing and building his own blue box. Others had used recordings on cassette tapes or their own whistles to capture the lines, but he wanted to use the digital chips that were coming out of the companies around him to make it work.

They also began looking for a character in the *Esquire* story. "Captain Crunch," one of the pioneers of the technology, had adopted the handle after learning that the plastic whistle inside the Cap'n Crunch cereal box, if blown properly, could hit just the right frequency to take over a long distance call. Through an acquaintance, Jobs and Wozniak tracked him down and invited him to meet.

The man who appeared at Wozniak's dorm-room door was no dashing captain. His hair was hanging to one side, some of his teeth were missing, and because he was living in his Volkswagen van, he hadn't showered in some time. Over several hours, they learned more details of how they could use the box, trading dialing codes and techniques.

Late that night, Wozniak and Jobs were heading back to Jobs's house in Los Altos when the little red Fiat broke down. Locating a pay phone, they asked an operator to dial an 800 number, intending to use the blue box to call for assistance.

But the phone company operator sniffed trouble and kept breaking into the call. Just as they were putting real money in the pay phone to make a legal call, a police car pulled up.

The police patted both of them down. One pulled the box from Wozniak's coat pocket and asked what it was. Wozniak told him it was a music synthesizer, a relatively new invention. As the police quizzed them, the pair grew increasingly nervous. Their answers apparently were satisfactory, however, and the police gave them a ride to a gas station and handed back the box.

Initially, Wozniak and Jobs used the box for their own amusement. Jobs used it to make calls from the school pay phone, for instance, to call a dial-a-joke line in Great Britain. He left a note on the phone for classmates to "listen, but don't hang up." One very late night, Wozniak even called the Vatican. Pretending to be Henry Kissinger, then President Richard Nixon's national security adviser, he asked to speak to the pope. Initially, the person on the other end said someone would be sent to wake him up—but then wised up when the caller couldn't control his laughter.

Despite the brush with the law, Jobs soon had a brainstorm. "Let's sell these," he told Wozniak. As orders came in, Wozniak figured out how to drive the cost of parts down from $80 to $40, and they sold boxes for $150 to students and $300 to others. With Wozniak taking the phreak handle

"Berkeley Blue" and Jobs adopting "Oaf Tobark," they made a tidy profit.

Then one summer evening, the two went to meet a potential customer. They were making their pitch when the customer pulled out a gun and aimed it at Jobs. Quickly realizing that nothing good would come from arguing, Jobs handed over the box.

Shortly after, he decided to get out of the business. He was getting bored with it, and the combined risk of getting shot or getting caught selling something illegal was too great. Wozniak, however, continued, and ultimately sold about two hundred boxes. Even after Jobs dropped out, Wozniak split his profit equally with his friend, just as they had done at the beginning.

The experience may have had one unexpected and long-lasting result. Ron Rosenbaum, who wrote that 1971 *Esquire* story, said later that Jobs's and Wozniak's early connection to the notorious outlaw Captain Crunch—whose real name was John Draper—may have been one reason that years later, computer hackers concentrated on computers made by other companies and left the Apple Macintosh alone.

As his time in high school grew shorter, Jobs began to rebel against traditional expectations. He perfected an unblinking stare that could unnerve people. He began to experiment with fasting and rigid diets, such as eating only fruits and vegetables. Jobs experimented with LSD with his first girlfriend, Chrisann Brennan. Also known as acid, LSD is an illegal drug that is considered highly dangerous today; forty years ago, it wasn't uncommon to meet people who had experimented with it in an effort to reach a deeper form of consciousness.

At seventeen, Jobs was skinny, with long hair, a scraggly beard, and a significant amount of angst. "He shuffled around and looked half-mad," Brennan said. But when they were together, he was quiet, shy, and funny, a romantic teenager who loved poetry, Dylan, and strumming his guitar. "He told me on our first or second date that he would be a millionaire someday, and I believed him," she said. "Steve could see the future."

At the end of the school year, Jobs decided he would spend the summer with Brennan in a cabin overlooking the Valley, to his father's dismay. Though the landlord initially turned him down, Jobs wasn't one to take no for an answer and the landlord finally rented them a room. Jobs and Brennan spent much of the summer there. His father had told him he couldn't—but as he had so many times, Jobs did it anyway, without any consequences. His dad even came to his rescue when the red Fiat caught fire.

To earn some money to fix the car and make ends meet, Jobs, Brennan, Wozniak, and another friend landed well-paying jobs as *Alice in Wonderland* characters at a local mall.

Brennan was Alice and the guys took turns playing the Mad Hatter and the White Rabbit, donning huge heads that reached to their knees. The weather was steamy, the mall's air conditioner was broken, and the costumes were heavy. Regularly, the men would run to the dressing room to get water and trade heads.

Wozniak thought it was fun, but not Jobs. "The costumes weighed a ton. After about four hours, you'd want to wipe out some kids," he said.

The misery was short-lived. Summer was ending and Jobs would head to college soon, just as his parents had promised so many years before. But the strong-willed young man would soon be doing things his own way once again.

Reed College.

4

College

Clara and Paul Jobs took their promise to send their son to college seriously, and they had socked some money away over the years. But they had never made much to begin with, and there was only so much they could save. Their son didn't see the situation the same way.

When the time came to apply for colleges, Jobs wasn't interested in the many campuses of the University of California, though a public university like Berkeley would have been much cheaper. Several of his classmates headed to Stanford and he could have gotten a scholarship there. But he rejected that idea, too, concluding that it was too staid for him and a better fit for young people who knew where they were going.

After visiting a friend at Reed College, a small, private, liberal arts school in Portland, Oregon, he found a fit. Reed

College had a student body of about twelve hundred—far smaller than Homestead High—and had a reputation for attracting free-thinkers and seekers. Jobs set his heart on going there and was admitted. But Reed's tuition and fees for the 1972–73 school year were $3,950 (about $21,400 in today's dollars), and that was simply more than his parents could afford to pay.

His father was aghast at the cost and tried to change his son's mind. His mother tried as well. But ultimately, they lost that battle as they had so many others. "Steve said that was the only college he wanted to go to, and if he couldn't go there, he didn't want to go anywhere," Clara Jobs said.

So, again, his parents gave in and scraped together the money for the first semester.

That fall, they packed the family car and drove Jobs to school. Ready to create a new life for himself, he didn't even give them the pleasure of a fond parting. "I sort of said, 'Well, thanks, bye.' I didn't even want the buildings to see that my parents were there," he said. "I just wanted to be like an orphan from Kentucky who had bummed around the country hopping freight trains for years."

Later, he said that he truly regretted his behavior that day. "It's one of the things in life I really feel ashamed about," he told a biographer. "I hurt their feelings. I shouldn't have. They had done so much to make sure I could go there."

Jobs almost immediately set about creating a most unusual college experience—but it didn't necessarily involve classes. Reed had demanding academic standards and required its freshmen to plow through a serious reading list the first semester. He expected a looser culture. When his friend Wozniak came to visit, he complained bitterly, "They are making me take all these courses."

Wozniak had hardly been a stellar college student himself, but at least he understood how the game was played. "Yes," Wozniak told him, "that's what they do in college."

Jobs would have nothing of it. He signed up for a dance class, mostly to meet girls. He stood out on campus for going almost everywhere barefoot, only slipping into sandals when it snowed. He and a new friend Daniel Kottke pursued their own reading list of books about Zen Buddhism, spirituality, enlightenment, and consciousness-raising. They practiced meditation and read *Diet for a Small Planet*. Both became committed vegetarians.

Jobs also became enthralled with a campus leader named Robert Friedland, who had served two years in prison for possession of LSD. Charismatic and a salesman, Friedland also provided LSD for Jobs's continued efforts, along with his diets and his extensive reading, to find greater personal enlightenment. Many years later, Jobs would tell a reporter that taking the psychedelic drug was one of the two or three most important things he had done in his life, changing him in ways that even those who knew him very well couldn't understand.

The relationship with Friedland changed Jobs, too. When Jobs arrived on campus, Kottke remembered, he was extremely shy and quiet. Friedland, by contrast, was fast-talking and glib, and always the center of attention. Inspired by Friedland's charm and salesmanship, Jobs began to open up and to take charge of situations. "After he spent time with Robert, some of it started to rub off," Kottke said.

For his part, Friedland was impressed with Jobs's intensity and his habit of staring at people and drilling them with questions, his eyes boring into the subject. He described Jobs as "one of the freaks of the campus."

Jobs was also taken with the visitors to Reed, including Richard Alpert, author of a favorite Jobs's book *Be Here Now,* who later became known as Ram Dass, and Timothy Leary, a former Harvard professor and proponent of psychedelic drugs, who was most famous for a mantra of the time, "Turn on, tune in, drop out."

"There was a constant flow of intellectual questioning about the truth of life," Jobs said.

With the Vietnam War winding down, the draft of twenty-year-old men into the military would end in December 1972, allowing the current generation to turn their focus inward, away from the long civil-rights and antiwar fights that had consumed their older brothers and sisters.

Given the choices Jobs was making, however, Jobs's parents weren't very happy with him. His grades weren't good, and they weren't paying all that tuition so their son could enjoy a hippie lifestyle.

Weighing the situation, Jobs decided to drop out of Reed at the end of his first semester.

It was another dot in the series of connections in his life, one that connected back to when he was born and that would connect forward into his future. His parents had kept their promise even though the cost of Reed was draining their savings. But since Jobs didn't have any idea what he wanted to do, he began to question if the price was worth it.

While dropping out was frightening at first, Jobs told the Stanford graduates that, in retrospect, "it was one of the best decisions I ever made." Liberated from all the required classes, he was now free to pursue whatever caught his fancy.

Because he wasn't paying for a dorm room, he slept on the floor of friends' rooms or found empty rooms that other disenchanted students used to occupy. He had impressed the dean of students with his "very inquiring mind," and the dean tacitly allowed him to hang around and attend classes.

Jobs collected soft drink bottles for the nickel deposit, which helped buy food. He told the Stanford graduates that he "would walk the seven miles across town every Sunday night to get one good meal a week at the Hare Krishna temple." Actually, he and Friedland often hitchhiked together, sometimes accompanied by Kottke and Kottke's girlfriend. There, they would dance and sing and then enjoy the free vegetable curry dinners.

Jobs also began to adopt even more bizarre diets. For a few weeks, he ate nothing more than Roman Meal whole-grain cereals topped with milk from the campus cafeteria. Then he became obsessed with the writings of a nineteenth-century Prussian who preached that certain foods created mucus and other wastes that damaged the body's functions. In his "typically nutso way," Jobs chided friends for eating bagels, dropped cereal from his personal menu, and began to subsist only on fruits or vegetables. He experimented with fasts that lasted from days to a couple of weeks and then were broken with water and leafy vegetables. At one point, he ate so many carrots, his friends said, that his skin turned "the color of an early sunset."

He spent weekends at a farm owned by Friedland's family, which became something of a commune. Jobs was in charge of keeping the apple orchards in good shape so the farm could make and sell organic cider, which, if handled right, fermented into an alcoholic hard cider. Others would cook up vegetarian feasts. A friend remembers that Jobs devoured them, but then forced himself to purge. "For years I thought he was bulimic," she said.

When the first school year ended and the dorms closed, Jobs rented an unheated room near campus for $25 a month. At one point, he borrowed money from a school fund and then got a job maintaining equipment for the psychology department's animal experiments. When Woz visited, they sold some blue boxes. (The users were caught and punished, but Jobs was not.) Chrisann Brennan came to visit occasionally as well.

His room could be cold and money was tight. But Jobs told the Stanford graduates of his freewheeling college time, "I loved it." He was free to explore whatever he found intriguing—and to his surprise, some of it would pay off many years later.

Among other things, he dropped into a calligraphy class. Elegant and elaborate hand lettering was featured around campus on posters, flyers, and even drawer labels. Jobs was fascinated by it and wanted to learn more. The class taught him about various fonts, serif and san serif type, and how letters are spaced. It seemed frivolous at the time, but fun.

To Kottke, Jobs was a driven young man, though his mission was far from clear. Perhaps it reflected some deep-seated insecurity. Perhaps it went back to his adoption. Whatever it was, Jobs "needs to prove himself to the world. He was waiting for the right crusade," he said.

By early 1974, about a year and a half after arriving at Reed, the crusade hadn't presented itself and Jobs was ready to move on. He wanted to travel to India but he didn't have any money. So, he returned home to a murky and uncertain future.

A College Reading List

In the 1970s, tiny Reed College in Portland, Oregon, attracted a mix of free spirits, artists, filmmakers, and poets, and unconventional thinkers, like the poet Allen Ginsberg and the author Ken Kesey.

But despite the liberal approach, professors expected students to read and think deeply, with a first semester reading list that included books like *The Iliad* and *The Peloponnesian Wars*.

Jobs, however, was more interested in seeking a different kind of understanding through Zen Buddhism, Eastern mysticism, and diet. These were among the books that made up his own personal reading list during his brief time at Reed:

Be Here Now *by Richard Alpert (now Ram Dass)*
Autobiography of a Yogi *by Paramahansa Yogananda*
Cosmic Consciousness *by Richard Maurice Bucke*
Cutting Through Spiritual Materialism *by Chögyam Trungpa*
Diet for a Small Planet *by Frances Moore Lappé*
Meditation in Action *by Chögyam Trungpa*
The Mucusless Diet Healing System *by Arnold Ehret*
Rational Fasting *by Arnold Ehret*
Zen Mind, Beginner's Mind *by Shunryu Suzuki*

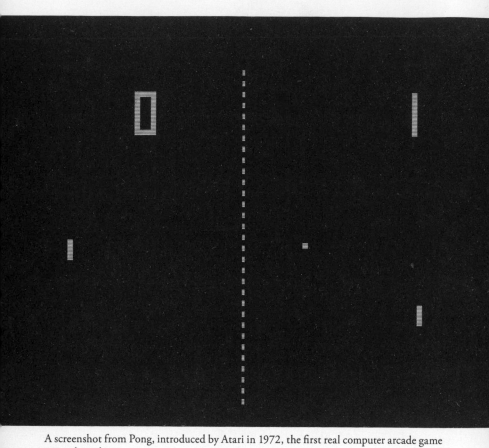

A screenshot from Pong, introduced by Atari in 1972, the first real computer arcade game ever released.

5

Searching

Back in his parents' home, Jobs perused the newspaper and saw an intriguing help-wanted ad: "Have fun and make money." Atari, an early maker of video games, was looking for technicians.

Jobs's main qualification was that he spent plenty of quarters playing Pong. The simplistic game, in which players moved horizontal lines, representing paddles, to bounce an electronic ball back and forth—a very crude electronic Ping-Pong—was Atari's first product and the first real video arcade game. Introduced in 1972, it was a huge hit. The success of Pong established the company as something of a creative leader in video games played in bars, bowling alleys, and pool halls. Atari also began making video games to be played on the home television.

Determined to earn enough to travel and unfazed by his

own lack of experience, Jobs showed up in the company's lobby with his long hair and ratty clothes, and announced that he wouldn't leave until he was hired. The chief engineer, Al Alcorn, chatted with him and saw "there was some spark, some inner energy" that convinced him to give the nineteen-year-old college dropout a job.

Many of Atari's other employees had long hair, were dropouts, or were serious off-road bikers, but even among that crowd, Jobs was a bit too offbeat. He rankled coworkers with his strong opinions and pointed criticism of their work. Worse, he had come to believe that his diet of yogurt and fruit meant he no longer had to shower regularly, which made him unpleasant to be around. Simply put, he smelled bad.

Alcorn moved Jobs to the night shift, where he could do his work refining and improving games without offending his coworkers.

After just a few months, Jobs told his Atari bosses that he planned to quit to go to India on a spiritual mission. Despite Jobs's efforts, the company wasn't interested in paying for his trip, but Alcorn generously offered to get him partway. Atari was having a technical problem in Germany that the German distributor couldn't fix. The company would send Jobs to take care of the problem, and he could travel to India from there.

"Say hi to the guru for me," Alcorn added.

In Germany, Jobs took care of the problem, but not before the Germany office complained about his prickly nature and odd smell. For his part, Jobs wasn't too thrilled about the meat and potatoes they wanted to feed him.

After a stop in Zurich, Switzerland, he flew to New Delhi, where he almost immediately came down with dysentery, running a high fever and dropping weight. When he felt better, he ventured north and happened on a religious festival. "I could smell good food. I hadn't been fortunate enough to smell good food for a long time, so I wandered up to pay my respects and eat some lunch," he recalled.

He apparently stood out in the crowd. While he was eating, the holy man of the festival spotted him and sat down next to him, laughing. Unable to communicate well, the holy man grabbed Jobs's arms and led him up a mountain trail to an area with a well and a small pond. There, the holy man dunked Jobs's head in water, pulled out a razor, and shaved his head, saying it was for the young man's health.

By the time Kottke showed up to travel with him, Jobs was thin, nearly bald, and wearing lightweight cotton garb. The pair rode rickety buses, negotiated at markets, and hiked along dried riverbeds. Though he was searching for a deeper spiritual awareness, Jobs was struck by the juxtaposition of extreme poverty and religious holiness. The pair sought out a guru that Friedland had told them about after a trip the year before. But the guru had died and everyone had scattered, leaving behind little more than plastic religious trinkets.

They continued their journey, contracting scabies in a town known for its spa. After he battled lice and fleas, Kottke cut his hair off as well. Ultimately, Jobs concluded, "We weren't going to find a place where we could go for a month to be enlightened." Having just come from a job in technology, he began to think that "maybe Thomas Edison did a lot more to improve the world" than any theorist or religious guru. After several months, he and Kottke returned to northern California, moved by the intense experience.

Years later, Jobs said that his experience in India taught him "the power of intuition and experiential wisdom," of relying on your experience and common sense, as opposed to Western intellect and rational thinking—a difference of approach that influenced his life's work. Even so, as Jobs moved out of his teens and into his third decade, he was still searching for something bigger.

For the next year or so, he alternated between his somewhat traditional life in Silicon Valley—working at Atari, auditing a Stanford physics class, and studying at a local Zen center—and his unusual Oregon lifestyle. With his college friends, he periodically stayed and worked at the Friedland farm, now the All One Farm commune. He began to seek information about his birth parents, learning that they had been unwed graduate students. He also paid $1,000 for a twelve-week course at the Oregon Feeling Center, which was supposed to address deep-seated problems from childhood through primal-scream therapy. Ultimately, he decided that wasn't the answer he was looking for, either.

In the summer of 1975, he was back at Atari, working nights as a consultant, when company founder, Nolan Bushnell, gave him a special assignment. Bushnell, a thirty-three-year-old entrepreneur who had taken a liking to Jobs, asked him to design a game called Breakout in which players destroy a brick wall with a bouncing ball. Because games in those days were programmed into the chips, not written as separate software like they are today, Bushnell wanted as few chips as possible in the design, and he wanted it fast. Actually, really fast: He wanted it done in four days.

Jobs was also spending time with his old high school friend Steve Wozniak, who had dropped out of college again to earn money and was now working at a dream job for Hewlett-Packard in the calculator business. Wozniak wasn't interested in mind-altering drugs, but he was hopelessly addicted to an Atari arcade game called Gran Trak 10 and Jobs was regularly letting his friend into the Atari office at night, where Woz could play the first video game with a steering wheel to his heart's content. There was another benefit: He could help Jobs if he got stuck on something.

Knowing the design work was beyond his skills, Jobs recruited Wozniak to figure out the chips and design, promising he would split the $700 he was being paid for the project. Working through the night after he got off his Hewlett-Packard job, Wozniak crafted the design using a minimum number of chips, and Jobs incorporated them into a prototype board. Bushnell, who would later found the Chuck E. Cheese pizza chain, was so pleased with the design he paid Jobs a bonus, reported to be $5,000. He also offered Wozniak a job.

Jobs paid Woz—but just the $350 he was promised at the start—and headed back to Oregon. The two both paid a price for their intense work; they both came down with the energy-sapping virus mononucleosis.

When the amount of the bonus Bushnell gave Jobs was disclosed in a book about Atari's history ten years later, long after the pair had founded Apple, Wozniak was truly hurt. He felt his good friend hadn't been honest and had betrayed him.

When Jobs heard about the book, he called his old friend and told him that he didn't remember keeping a bonus, and since he surely would have remembered it, "he probably didn't do it."

Many years later, when Jobs's biographer Walter Isaacson quizzed Jobs about the payment, "he became unusually quiet and hesitant. 'I don't know where that allegation comes from,' he said. 'I gave him half the money I ever got.'"

Still, both Bushnell and Alcorn remember that a bonus was paid—and Woz is sure he received only $350. It was an ugly side of Steve Jobs, the charmer who sometimes only took care of himself.

In many ways, it was fortunate that Wozniak didn't know the whole story when it happened. He had been attending meetings of a new computer club and was so intrigued that he was soon trying to design his own computer. He couldn't help but share his ideas with his good friend and recent collaborator Steve Jobs.

What came next would change both of their lives. It would also change the world.

Steve Wozniak (left) and Steve Jobs working on the Apple I in 1976.

6

Apple

To say that Steve Wozniak was wowed with the idea of a computer in a small box might be an understatement.

At the least, he was incredibly inspired by the idea and couldn't wait to try it out.

In January 1975, *Popular Electronics* ran a cover story on the first real "micro" computer, the Altair, made by a company out of Albuquerque, New Mexico. It was a kit, really, which took hours to assemble and didn't really work very well once it was together. It didn't come with any other accessories—no screen, no keyboard, not even a way to talk to it. To use it, a hobbyist had to write a program, and even then, about all the Altair could do was blink back with the lights on the front of the box. In many ways, it was surprisingly similar to the Cream Soda Computer that Wozniak had shown off to Steve Jobs nearly five years before.

But there was one huge difference inside. While Wozniak had been focusing on calculators at Hewlett, running a dial-a-joke service from his home, and dating his first girlfriend, the power and abilities of semiconductors had exploded. Starting in the late 1950s, engineers had figured out how to combine many transistors on a small slice of silicon, along with the connections between them. These new integrated circuits, or microchips, could hold chunks of memory or handle other tasks, taking over whole sections of a computer. But the circuits were hardwired into the chips, meaning the chips could only do what they were programmed to do—like Jobs's and Wozniak's version of Breakout.

In the early 1970s, however, a young Silicon Valley company called Intel Corporation developed a single chip that could actually be programmed to perform all kinds of new and different functions. This so-called microprocessor, the size of a fingertip, combined several functions into one and could be the entire central processing unit, or CPU, of a computer—the brains inside the box. And it could be driven by software, special programs written to specifically teach it to complete many kinds of tasks. As Intel improved on its microprocessor, allowing it to work faster and handle more information at one time, the idea of a microcomputer, a true "personal" computer, became a reality.

Wozniak got his first whiff of these huge developments

when he attended the initial meeting of the Homebrew Computer Club in a Menlo Park, California, garage that March. It was a cold and drizzly evening, but many of the thirty people who showed up were buzzing about the Altair and the possibilities of a small computer. Someone passed out a data sheet on a competing microprocessor.

Wozniak took the sheet home and studied the details of this new kind of chip. Suddenly, he had a revelation. "It was as if my whole life had been leading up to this point," he said later. All those times he had drawn sketches of redesigned minicomputers, the crude Cream Soda Computer, his work on video games—all of that had led him to this very opportunity. "That night, the night of that first meeting, this whole vision of a kind of personal computer just popped into my head. All at once. Just like that."

Right away, he began sketching a design.

Conceptualizing his new computer turned out to be much easier than building it. The fabulous Intel chip, it turned out, cost about $400, "almost more than my monthly rent," he said. In addition, he would need memory chips, a language for communicating with the chips, and other pieces. It would take time and money to pull it all together.

Early on, Wozniak discovered that Hewlett-Packard employees could get a discount on a Motorola microprocessor with the same potential as the Intel one. And then he found an even cheaper alternative, a $20 knock-off from a little-known company that would run his design exactly as he'd conceived it. He had made the decision based on economics, not on engineering, and it would turn out to be a significant—and potentially foolish—one. Nearly every other computer would be designed on the Intel chip, which was different enough that every piece of software that talked to it would have to be different, too.

Wozniak's friend Steve Jobs went to a few Homebrew meetings, carrying in Woz's television set so that he could demonstrate his latest development on the television screen. But Jobs found the geeky conversation of the every-other-week gatherings tedious. The club was so nerdy, Wozniak once joked, that "you could have called it 'Chips and Dips.'" Still, every time the two chatted on the phone or got together, they discussed the computer and Wozniak's progress.

By late June, Wozniak had a breakthrough: He had pulled together chips, a power supply, a monitor, and a keyboard. The first time he typed on the keyboard, letters popped up on the monitor, just like they were supposed to. It was a "Eureka!" moment.

Had it been left fully to Wozniak, he would have given away all of his designs and details to members of the club, whose motto was "Give help to others." But Jobs, admiring his friend's clever work and seeing a bigger opportunity, encouraged him to stop sharing so much with the club, which had ballooned to several hundred members.

Later that year, Jobs made a proposal. Many of the hobbyists showing up to the club had ideas, but not enough time to carry them through. So, he suggested he and Wozniak could sell printed circuit boards to them and the members could just plug in their own chips, a much simpler process than designing boards themselves.

Wozniak was skeptical that there would be much interest—or that the two could earn back the $1,000 it would cost. But Jobs, who still hadn't figured out what he really wanted to do with his life, was persistent, telling him, "Well, even if we lose our money, we'll have a company."

Wozniak gave in, and the two began to scrounge up their initial investment. Wozniak sold his H-P calculator for $500—but the buyer ultimately paid him only half that. Jobs sold his red-and-white Volkswagen bus, but he had to spend some of his profit on repairing the bus after it broke down shortly after the sale. Together, they managed to raise about $1,300, equal to about $5,000 today.

Next, they needed a name for their partnership. On the way back from the airport after Wozniak picked up Jobs from another trip to the All One Farm, Jobs threw out a suggestion: Apple Computer.

After all, he had just come back from the apple orchard

and he was in one of his fruitarian stages, eating a lot of apples. Even better, the name would put them near the top of any alphabetical list—and ahead of Atari in the phone book. They tried to come up with something better, like Matrix Electronics or Executek. But Apple just seemed to fit.

Both fretted, however, that they might run afoul of the Beatles, the famous quartet known for its Apple record label. (That turned out to be a real concern.) And Jobs worried that maybe Apple was too cutesy for a company that wanted to be taken seriously. But unable to come up with anything better, they went ahead with it.

Jobs convinced Ron Wayne, a former boss from the night shift at Atari, to create a logo and draw up what went where—the schematics—of the circuit board. Wayne produced an elaborate etching of Newton under a tree, with a glowing apple overhead.

As they moved forward, Wozniak began to sweat about the consequences. What if he had to use some of his ideas for Apple in his job at Hewlett-Packard? What if he wanted to share his ideas some other way? To clear his conscience, Wozniak also told his bosses at H-P that he had come up with a design for a small, inexpensive computer.

A meeting was set up with some H-P managers, and Wozniak presented his computer. The higher-ups were interested, but they couldn't envision it as a product for H-P. They told Wozniak that the company wasn't interested.

Wozniak was disappointed, but he could now pursue the computer on his own. He and Jobs agreed to split their share equally. But sensing that they also needed a tie-breaker, they made Wayne a partner, too, giving him a 10 percent stake, while they each received 45 percent.

Wayne drew up an agreement, and on April 1, 1976, the three signed it, officially creating Apple Computer.

The arrangement would be short-lived. Wayne was in his forties and much more conservative than his twenty-something partners. He already had suffered big losses when he tried to start a slot-machine company and failed. Now, if Apple ran into trouble, he would be on the hook again. Reflecting on that, he got cold feet. "I had already learned what gave me indigestion," he said. "If Apple had failed, I would have had bruises on top of bruises. Steve Jobs was an absolute whirlwind and I had lost the energy you need to ride whirlwinds."

Shortly after he signed, he pulled out of the partnership, receiving $800 for his share. Later, just to be sure everything was kosher, Apple would pay him another $1,700. That was good enough for him. (Had he stayed on, however, and held on to his piece of the company until today, he would have become a billionaire.)

Jobs and Wozniak would soon be too busy to think about the setback. Trying to drum up sales for the one hundred circuit boards he had ordered, Jobs strolled barefoot into a new computer store called the Byte Shop and began to pitch Paul Terrell, the owner and a Homebrew Computer Club regular. Terrell was trying to build a chain to rival RadioShack, and he quickly got to the point with the aggressive young salesman: He didn't want circuit boards and neither did his customers. A computer store needed computers. And if little Apple wanted to provide him with fully built computers, he would buy fifty of them at about $500 each—in cash.

Jobs was stunned. He had been looking to sell some $50 circuit boards, and now he had a $25,000 order in hand. Dollar signs flashed in front of his eyes.

He called Wozniak right away. "Are you sitting down?" he asked.

Wozniak was shocked—astounded, really. The order was for roughly his annual salary, far more than he could have ever imagined.

But the tiny company had no parts, no money to buy them, and no place to put the computers together. How would it ever deliver?

Apple vs. Apple

Steve Jobs and Steve Wozniak were right to worry about whether naming their new company Apple would cause trouble with the Beatles' company, Apple Corps.

The pair was way too inexperienced and naïve to hire a lawyer to formally investigate the question. But, in fact, their decision did spark a long-running feud between two of the world's biggest Apples.

Once Apple Computer began getting attention, Apple Corps sued it. In a 1981 settlement, Apple Computer agreed to stick to computers, leaving the music to Apple Corps. But the settlement didn't buy any love between the two.

In the late 1980s, former Beatle George Harrison saw that the Macintosh computer could be used to compose music and could include a device that would allow musicians to program instruments. Unable to let it be, Apple Corps sued again.

After a months-long trial, the two sides reached a new settlement, with Apple Computer paying an estimated $26.5 million to resolve the issue.

The creation of the iTunes store in 2003 reopened the old wound and led to yet another lawsuit. Showing that they can work it out, the two reached a final agreement in 2007, giving Apple control of all the trademarks, some of which it licensed back to the Beatles' Apple Corps.

Even so, Beatles music wasn't available on iTunes until 2010.

It was, as way too many stories noted over the years, a long and winding road.

Steve Jobs's childhood home in Los Altos, California, and the garage where Apple Computer first launched.

7

Garage

To build a company, even a small one, you need money. So Jobs first went looking for cash, or at least someone willing to let him purchase parts that he would pay for later.

•　He approached a bank for a loan. He tried to get a credit line at his old parts store. He asked his old Atari bosses if he could purchase parts from them.

They all said no.

Finally, Wozniak got a small loan from some friends and Jobs convinced a chip distributor to sell them the parts on credit. Apple would have thirty days to pay, or it would be charged interest. It was a typical business arrangement, but Jobs didn't know that.

The next problem was finding a place to build the new computer. Wozniak, now twenty-five and recently married, was working from his cramped apartment, and his wife, Alice, was growing frustrated. Her husband was always working, either at Hewlett-Packard or on the new computer, and her dining table was covered with stuff that couldn't be disturbed.

Jobs, now twenty-one, was living at home again. He took over his sister Patty's old bedroom, organizing the parts in a chest of drawers there. He also recruited Patty, who was married and expecting her first child, to plug all the parts into the new printed circuit boards, paying her $1 a board. Between work in his bedroom and her old one, the first machines came together.

When Jobs proudly delivered the first dozen computers to the Byte Shop, however, Terrell was unimpressed. There was no keyboard, no power source, no screen—there wasn't even a case around it. Nor was there a computer language to make it work. But Terrell, true to his word, paid Jobs for it and assembled the missing pieces himself.

With the very first profits, Jobs rented a post-office box and lined up an answering service, both intended to make Apple look like a real company. By the time the first fifty crude computers were built and sold to Terrell, Apple had enough profit—money left over after its expenses—to pay for parts for fifty more computers. Feeling like he was on a roll, Jobs was sure he could sell more computers to friends and other stores.

To help, Jobs recruited his old high school friend Bill

Fernandez, who had been working at Hewlett-Packard. A college friend was hired to keep the books, and when Daniel Kottke joined the business for the summer, he took over the Jobs's family couch.

As the house became increasingly crowded, Jobs's dad, Paul, decided the business needed to move. So he replanted the sprouting enterprise in his beloved garage. He put up plasterboard and added lighting and a phone line. He moved his car parts outside, set aside his own tools, and turned the space over to his son.

Even Jobs's mom, Clara, was sucked into the business, answering the phone, welcoming salespeople and potential customers, and putting up with her son's crazy fruit and carrot diets and Wozniak's junk-food wrappers. At one point, journalist Michael Moritz wrote, Clara and Paul told friends jokingly that they "were paying the mortgage in exchange for kitchen, bathroom, and bedroom privileges."

With its initial sales, Apple even got its first press. In July 1976, *Interface* magazine reported that Jobs, who had been "a private consultant to Atari," was director of marketing, and Wozniak, "the creative and innovative talent," was director of engineering. The "core" of the company, it said with some overstatement, was "a well-disciplined, financially sound group that is opening new vistas in computer hardware, software, and service to their clientele."

The clatter from the Jobs garage was sounding like a real company.

Despite the sales of the new computer, Jobs was in a quandary. He was still looking for some deeper meaning in his life, and he seriously considered packing up and going to a Zen monastery in Japan.

He had been visiting his old girlfriend Chrisann Brennan at the Zen Center and became a regular there himself. He shared his concerns with Kobun Chino, a spiritual adviser with whom Jobs would remain close, and Chino listened. Finally, he told Jobs to stay with his business, that it would be just as meaningful as a monastery. And after some hesitation, Jobs agreed.

While Jobs was weighing his future and overseeing the manufacture, sales, and marketing of the first computer, Wozniak had already started on another computer, tailored to his favorite things. He figured out a way to make the computer generate color so he could show it off on a color television. Because he wanted to play the Atari Breakout game on his new toy, he added sound, graphics, and the ability to add a device you could hold in your hand so you could move the paddles on the screen. Because many of the chips supporting the microprocessor were getting faster and more able, he could make the computer faster and sharper, too. And because Wozniak loved to come up with designs that were sleek and efficient, he was able to cut the number of chips in half compared with the first version.

He even built the BASIC language into the system, so that a buyer could bring it home, hook up a television set or monitor, turn it on, and actually write programs for it right away.

As he finished up his design, he and Jobs tangled over one detail: Woz wanted eight extra slots that buyers could use to add equipment or an extra circuit board. Jobs wanted to limit the number to two, assuming people would only want a printer and maybe a modem, a device for allowing the computer to talk through a phone line. He wanted to keep it simple.

The argument dragged on. But Wozniak, knowing how potential computer buyers would want to tinker with and improve on their purchases, stood his ground, and actually won Jobs over.

The Apple I was for hobbyists and geeks. But *this* computer would be for people who wanted a computer to do something.

To see what other innovations were being nurtured in the small-computer nursery, Jobs and Wozniak flew to Atlantic City at the end of August 1976 to attend a computer show. They kept their newest computer under wraps in the hotel room, and tried to sell a few Apple Is. While Wozniak worked on the new computer in the hotel room, Jobs studied the competition, companies with forgettable names like IMSAI, Cromemco, and Processor Technology. He heard that RadioShack was considering making its own computer, as was Commodore, a maker of calculators. He came away with two conclusions: Apple had a better machine than all of them, but it needed to be a lot better looking.

To make what Jobs and Wozniak began to call the Apple II, they would need a substantial amount of money—more than $100,000. Through Jobs's former boss Al Alcorn, Jobs got an audience with Atari's president. But Jobs's youth and inexperience showed. While trying to charm the executive and win his support, Jobs propped his bare feet up on the man's desk. The man got a front-row view of what accumulates when one doesn't wear shoes.

It was a deal-killer.

"Get your feet off my desk," he barked at the young entrepreneur, adding sharply, "we're not going to buy your product!"

On another stop, Jobs tried to negotiate with a distributor for a good price on memory chips. When his initial pitch didn't work, Jobs warned that he would yank his business from the company, even though he had never purchased anything from it before.

Wozniak, knowing that they needed the chips, started to interrupt. Jobs tried to shush his friend with a swift kick.

Instead of connecting, however, he slid off the chair and slipped under the table.

The salesman, appreciating the comedic touch, gave Apple a line of credit.

The search for financial support also brought a parade of money men to the Jobs' family garage. A top Commodore executive showed up in a suit and a cowboy hat and said he was interested in buying the company.

Jobs wanted a nice payday, and he told the Commodore folks that he believed the company was worth at least $100,000 (about $400,000 today). Further, he and Wozniak should both be hired at annual salaries of $36,000, far more than Wozniak was making at Hewlett-Packard. Ultimately, Commodore decided to build its own computer, a relief to Jobs, who came to believe the companies were a bad fit.

But the courting led to new tension between Jobs and his longtime partner. The Wozniak family had been skeptical of Jobs and his true intentions for some time. They were put off by his sloppy appearance and feared that he might be taking advantage of their son, who was brilliant with technology but socially immature. In the midst of Commodore's interest, the discussion about who deserved what credit—and money— turned ugly. Jerry Wozniak, Woz's dad, reduced Jobs to tears one day, telling him, "You haven't produced anything. You haven't done anything."

Jobs was hurt and told Wozniak that if they weren't equal partners, then Wozniak could have the whole thing.

But his old friend and collaborator knew better. Wozniak could design a circuit board and Jobs couldn't—but Jobs could get one hundred circuit boards printed, something Wozniak couldn't do. Woz could sketch out complex electronics and write software, but Jobs was the one who could get it made into a single product and sell it. True, Wozniak had invented the Apple computer, but he would have given it away. "It never crossed my mind to sell computers. It was Steve's idea to hold them in the air and sell a few," he said.

Each one needed the other. And they both knew it.

They also still needed funding. Jobs went to the Atari founder, Nolan Bushnell, who had sold the game maker to Warner Communications that year, clearing $14 million. Bushnell didn't want to invest, but he put Jobs in touch with a venture capitalist, an investor who put money in young companies in exchange for ownership.

Don Valentine arrived at the Jobs garage in his Mercedes-Benz. He had invested in Atari and knew about start-up companies in Silicon Valley, but these two kids struck him as naïve, especially when they told him that they might sell "a couple of thousand" computers a year. To them, that would have been a lot, since they had sold fewer than two hundred so far.

Valentine accurately concluded that they didn't know about marketing or how to win big sales. And, he said, "They weren't thinking anywhere near big enough." To him, that was a bad sign. "Big thinkers often do big things. Small thinkers never do big things," he liked to say. He turned them down, but gave

The cover for the Apple-1 operating manual features Apple's first logo, drawn by Ron Wayne in 1976.

Jobs the name of another potential investor, A. C. "Mike" Markkula.

Markkula, who was only in his early thirties, was an early employee of Intel and had become a millionaire when the chip company first sold stock to the public. He was now mostly retired, enjoying his family and living off his investments.

Markkula arrived at the Jobs garage in a gold Chevrolet Corvette sports car. First, he noticed that both Steves needed a haircut. Then, he saw the computer and was blown away. "It was what I had wanted since I left high school," he said. At that point, he forgot about appearances. "You can always get a haircut," he said.

After a series of discussions, he offered to personally guarantee a credit line of $250,000 to get the Apple II off the ground. He had one condition: Wozniak had to quit Hewlett-Packard and join the company full-time.

There was one hitch: Wozniak had no intention of doing that.

Not Yet Ripe

Much like early automobiles, the Apple I computer hardly bore a resemblance to what computers would become over the decade.

Apple's operations manual noted that it was fully assembled and tested. Owners only needed to install a keyboard, display, and power source. After attaching those, it recommended a simple test program to be sure everything was working properly. The instructions were hardly user friendly:

"FIRST: Hit the RESET button to enter the system monitor. A backslash should be displayed, and the cursor should drop to the next line.

SECOND: Type- Ø : A9 b Ø b AA b 2Ø b EF b FF b E8 b 8A b 4C b 2 b Ø (RET)

(Ø is zero, NOT an alpha 'O'; b means blank or space; and (RET) hit the "return" key on the keyboard)

THIRD: Type- Ø . A (RET)

(This should print out, on the display, the program you have just entered.)

FOURTH: Type- R (RET)

(R means run the program.)"

Once run, the program would spit out a stream of characters, showing that the keyboard, monitor, and computer were talking to each other. To stop the program, you needed to hit "reset."

Piece of cake, right?

Steve Jobs (left) and Steve Wozniak collaborating on the Apple II.

8

Apple II

If Steve Jobs wasn't thinking big enough, Mike Markkula definitely was.

A former marketing manager for Intel, Markkula had never run a company himself. But the one-time high school gymnast was a true engineer who appreciated the potential of desktop computers as much as anybody. He realized right away that the Apple II could be much more than a toy for hobbyists or game players. It could be a truly useful tool, especially for regular folks who wanted to keep track of recipes or a bank account.

"This is the start of an industry," he told Jobs and Wozniak, predicting the company would make the Fortune 500, the prestigious list of America's biggest companies, in a matter of years. "It happens once a decade."

To make it happen, he needed the right team—and that

included Steve Wozniak, as well as Steve Jobs. Wozniak, however, was plenty happy working for Hewlett-Packard, and his
young wife liked the security of the regular paycheck. Plus,
he had decided long before that he never wanted to tell people
what to do. He would rather design computers and write software. "I'm not a management person," he said.

He mulled over the choice for a few days and told Markkula that he would stay where he was.

Steve Jobs didn't like to take no for an answer, and he
didn't plan to start now. He went on a one-man crusade to
change his friend's mind. Jobs lobbied Wozniak's friends to
call him. He called Woz's brother, and even went to Wozniak's parents to tearfully beg them for help. Within a couple
of days, Woz's phone was ringing off the hook.

Ultimately, Jobs's campaign worked. A longtime friend
finally convinced Wozniak that he could make his fortune as
an engineer at the new company without having to become
a boss or an executive.

In January 1977, the Apple Computer Company was formally created, with Jobs, Wozniak, and Markkula owning
equal shares, and a bit of ownership reserved for others. To
finish his team, Markkula brought in an old friend and former coworker Mike Scott as president, who, as the second
"Mike" became known as "Scotty."

Scott's assignment was to bring some order to the ragtag
business and to keep Jobs more or less in line. But from the

start, the intense and sometimes temperamental Scott knocked heads with the passionate and often abrasive Jobs.

When Scott arrived, Apple had moved out of the garage and into its first office, and one of his first jobs was to create a proper payroll. Chris Espinosa, who was still attending Homestead High School at the time, had started out working in the garage over the winter holidays and recalled that Jobs "had been paying people out of the company checkbook, and not all that regularly." So on St. Patrick's Day, Scott assigned everyone an employee number for the payroll system, keeping no. 7 for himself. Espinosa, who still works for Apple, was no. 8 because the other numbers had been handed out by the time he got out of school.

Wozniak was given no. 1 and Jobs no. 2—a decision that sent Jobs into a furor. He confronted Scott and demanded no. 1. He threw a fit. But unlike so many other people Jobs encountered over the years, Scott wouldn't back down. He agreed to a minor compromise: Jobs put no. 0 on his employee badge, but remained no. 2 for payroll purposes.

While Wozniak worked on the new circuit board, Scott focused on the manufacturing, Markkula looked after the marketing and the money, and Jobs took over just about everything else to do with the office and the Apple II. He was notoriously fussy about the smallest details; when the office typewriter was delivered, he was furious that it was blue and not a more neutral color. When the phone company brought phones in the wrong color, he fussed until they were changed. He wanted white workbenches, not gray ones.

Jobs's greatest demands were for the computer itself. He rejected the first design for a printed circuit board because the lines weren't straight enough, even though the board would be invisible to computer owners. He hired a specialist to design a power supply that wouldn't need a noisy fan to keep it cool. While all the other computer makers were using metal cases, he decided a plastic case would be sleeker and more inviting.

In coming up with the concept for the case, Jobs studied the design of home appliances and stereos at a Macy's department store. He had dozens of shades of beige to choose from but he didn't really like any of them and wanted to create his own. He spent weeks debating exactly how rounded the edges of the case should be, nearly driving Scott crazy with his indecision.

Time magazine once said Wozniak was "the kind of guy who can see a sonnet in a circuit." Jobs, by contrast, could look at a beige box and see beauty. He imagined a computer that was as graceful and elegant as it was useful, an intersection of technology and art that resulted in something truly special. That vision would drive him, with varying degrees of success, for the rest of his career.

Still, his demands for perfection—as he defined it—were hard on the people around him. He wanted lower prices from every supplier, telling them, "You better sharpen your pencil." He belittled the work of young programmers, sometimes without fully understanding what they were doing, and he shared an opinion about everything. He and Scott yelled at each other so often and so publicly that people referred to their disagreements as the "Scotty Wars." Jobs had to be cooled down with walks around the parking lot.

"Jobs cannot run anything," Scott said. "After you get something started, he causes lots of waves. He likes to fly around like a hummingbird at ninety miles per hour."

For all Jobs's insistence that the computer's appearance be perfect, he didn't apply the same standard to himself. Among his more unusual habits was creating a makeshift foot massage: He sat on the toilet tank, put his feet in the bowl, and flushed to relieve stress. Jobs still wasn't bathing regularly and because of his diet, he didn't think he needed to. That made him truly unpleasant to be around. Both Scott and Markkula tried to get him to reconsider. "We would have to literally put him out the door and tell him to go take a shower," Markkula said. Even then, it would be some time before his grooming habits improved.

The West Coast held its first computer fair in the spring of 1977 and the early Apple employees rushed to get the new computer ready. When the first cases came back with tiny bubbles in the plastic, Jobs made sure they were sanded and painted to look good.

This time, Apple had rented a space near the front of the fair and was going first class. It had ordered a big sign with the company's new colorful Apple logo: an apple with a bite taken out—in part a wink at a computer "byte," the amount of computer storage needed to hold one letter. Apple's only three fully equipped Apple IIs were on display. More than thirteen thousand people attended the show and it's hard to know what was more impressive: that Steve Jobs bought and wore his first suit or that Apple took home three hundred orders for its $1,298 computer.

After bringing in almost nothing in the first four months of 1977, the little company sold $774,000 worth of computers by the end of September, and even recorded a profit of almost $42,000 in its first year as a real company.

But it wasn't much of a company, yet. It had a nice brochure, with a photo of a bright red apple and a slogan, "Simplicity is the ultimate sophistication." The offices were one big space, with no receptionist, no meeting rooms, and people rushing from one thing to another. Half the room was carpeted, and that was for sales, marketing, and the bosses. The other half had linoleum and six lab benches, for engineering and manufacturing.

Because no one else was available to talk with people who dropped by to learn more, Chris Espinosa came to the office on Tuesdays and Thursdays after school to demonstrate the computer to whoever wanted to see it.

Sales continued to grow, especially as people outside of Apple began to write and sell games and other programs on

Simplicity
is the
ultimate
sophistication.

Introducing
Apple II,
the personal
computer.

A brochure for the Apple II features one of Apple's first slogans: "Simplicity is the ultimate sophistication." This belief can still be seen in Apple's products, designs, and advertising campaigns today.

cassette tapes that allowed the computer to be more useful. Markkula had written a program to balance a bank account and he urged Wozniak to find a way to hook up a small disk drive that would allow the program to load onto the computer and run faster. By spring 1978, Wozniak had figured out how to get the Apple II to talk to a new disk drive that could read data from flat, flimsy, five-and-a-quarter-inch floppy disks.

Now, new software would be much easier to share, sell, and use. Apple's sales exploded to $7.9 million by the end of September 1978.

All along, Jobs and his partners at Apple thought they were building machines for hobbyists, game players, and home users. But in 1979, a couple of business types in Boston came up with a way to simplify financial calculations. Before that, every time one assumption about sales or costs changed, someone would have to recalculate dozens of numbers by hand to figure out the impact. Calling their program VisiCalc, for "visible calculator," they designed the program on the Apple II and sold it only for Apple computers. Now, business people, who had largely ignored these new desktop computers, had a really good reason to buy an Apple.

Benjamin Rosen, a stock analyst at Morgan Stanley in New York, wanted his tech department to buy him an Apple computer, but they didn't believe it would be useful. "It took just one demo," he remembered. He opened up VisiCalc and showed the techs rows and columns of financial numbers. He changed one of them, and hit "recalc." Every other number on the sheet was updated.

" 'Wow' resounded through the room," he said, and he got his computer, becoming one of the most vocal and visible supporters of the young company.

While Jobs worked long hours to stay up with Apple's growth, he was facing a different kind of challenge in his personal life. He and his old college friend Daniel Kottke rented a home they nicknamed Rancho Suburbia, and Jobs's on-and-off girlfriend Chrisann Brennan moved into one of the rooms, taking a job at Apple. The relationship picked back up for a time—until Brennan became pregnant.

Brennan was certain Jobs was the father. He denied it, and had no interest in getting married. He discouraged her from putting the baby up for adoption, but otherwise paid little attention, essentially ignoring her. Frustrated, angry, and not very stable emotionally, Brennan quit her job and moved to the All One Farm in Oregon that she had visited before.

The child, a little girl, was born there on May 17, 1978. Jobs came to visit her three days later, and together they named the girl Lisa Nicole Brennan. But after that, he didn't want anything to do with Brennan or the baby.

Though Jobs's slice of Apple was worth millions of dollars by then, he only occasionally provided any financial help and continued to deny that he was the father. At one point, he even signed a court document saying he wasn't physically able to have children. Meanwhile, Brennan worked at odd jobs and lived on county welfare payments.

In 1979, when DNA tests were new, Jobs surprised Brennan by agreeing to settle the matter once and for all. The paternity test concluded there was a 94.41 percent chance that he was the father. Still, he insisted to friends, people at Apple, and even reporters that, statistically, someone else could be the father.

Finally, the county of San Mateo sued Jobs and he was

ordered to pay $385 a month in child support and to repay the county $5,856 for welfare payments it had made.

"I could not see myself as a father then, so I didn't face up to it," he said. He later regretted his behavior, saying, "I wish I had handled it differently." Over time, he bought Chrisann a house, paid for Lisa's schools, and supported her financially. But it would be a long time before he would actually be anything like a father to Lisa.

In a strange twist of fate, Jobs was twenty-three when Lisa was born, the same age as his own biological parents when he was born outside of a marriage and put up for adoption. But he wouldn't know that for a few more years. For now, his attention was focused on his other baby, Apple, which was about to make him a very proud papa.

Computer Talk

To build his new computer, Wozniak needed more than a microprocessor. Here are some of the other components found in the Apple II—and many other computers:

ROM is read-only memory. This chip holds specialized, fixed information that can't be erased or changed. Once Wozniak wrote a language to work on the Apple, it was stored in the read-only memory so that it came up when the computer was turned on.

RAM is random-access memory. This memory is temporary and it can be erased and written over. When you open up new programs on your screen, your computer's RAM helps you do that. (That's also why you can lose your work if you don't save it regularly to a hard drive.)

With the Apple II, Wozniak became an early user of DRAM, or dynamic random-access memory, which requires continual electronic refreshing. DRAM chips are also smaller and cheaper than the old static random access memory (SRAM chips), meaning more could be used.

Wozniak's first Apple II had eight thousand bytes of DRAM. Today, most computer users want two to four *billion* bytes of memory so their computers will work quickly and smoothly.

BASIC is a simple computer language that allows people to write programs and software that tell the computer what to do. Just like we need words to communicate, a computer needs a language, too.

One of the early BASIC languages was written for the Altair by some Harvard kids, Bill Gates, Paul Allen, and Marty Davidoff, based on a BASIC language used by Digital Equipment Corporation. Gates and Allen would go on to start a company called Microsoft.

Wozniak wrote his BASIC for Apple based on an H-P version. Just as people in Texas speak differently than those in New York, the two versions of BASIC weren't the same. For a program written for the Apple to work on a computer running Gates's and Allen's BASIC, some translation would have to take place.

After Apple's success with the Apple II computer, Steve Jobs became something of a celebrity—appearing on the cover of several magazines as the face of the new personal computer revolution. *Inc.* was the first magazine cover Jobs appeared on.

9

Rich

As Steve Jobs discovered early on, every growing company needs money—a lot of it—to fuel its expansion. As Apple grew, it needed more engineers to design new products, more office space and manufacturing space, more parts and equipment, more advertising, and so on.

That fund-raising would change the direction of Apple and the lives of its founders.

Markkula's initial investment began to run low in late 1977, and the company raised its first funds from outsiders early the next year. With the introduction of the Apple II, the company that was valued at $5,309 when it was formed in early 1977 was valued at about $3 million just a year later. New investors would buy more shares in 1979 and 1980. Each time, they would pay more than the last bunch. Their purchases would reduce the percentage of ownership Jobs held, but since each investor paid more than the last, the value of his stock went up.

The result? By the time Jobs was twenty-three years old, he was worth more than $1 million. By the time he was twenty-four, he was worth more than $10 million. In 1979, he and Markkula each sold more than $1 million of their stock. Jobs cleaned up his act and traded in his torn jeans for tailored suits and, occasionally, bow ties. He traded his rental house for a home in Los Gatos and his clunkers for a Mercedes-Benz. But partly because he was so particular about design and appearances, he never really furnished his house, living for years with a mattress and Apple II on the floor of his bedroom and little more than a table and chairs.

One 1979 investor was the giant Xerox Corporation. As part of the purchase, Apple got a peek at some secret research Xerox had been doing at its nearby Palo Alto Research Center. At the time, computer screens were nothing more than black windows with white- or amber-colored ugly type. To play a game, you would insert the disk in the drive and type >RUN GAME, D1 and hit RETURN. Then, after much whirring and stopping, the game would load from the disk drive.*

---

* To get a sense what these screens looked like, click on the taskbar icon in the far left corner of a PC, type CMD in the box, and hit RETURN. A window will pop up that is similar to the way early computers looked.

At Xerox PARC, as the research center was called, scientists and engineers had been working for years on ways to make computers simpler and easier to use. While the desktop computer was still in its infancy, they were running networks of dozens of computers linked together and sharing e-mail, more than a decade before it became common for regular people. They were using a rolling rectangular box called a mouse, which sat next to the computer and helped the user navigate around the screen. They also had taken the idea of a desk, with its scattered papers and folders, and, in a fashion, re-created the look on a screen, calling each page a window and using folder images like real files in a file cabinet.

Jobs took one look and saw the future. His Xerox hosts remember him hopping up and down and shouting, "You're sitting on a gold mine!"

"It was one of those sort of apocalyptic moments," he said later. After seeing what Xerox called a graphical user interface (sometimes pronounced "gooey" after its GUI initials), he was certain that "every computer would work this way some day. It was so obvious once you saw it."

What was also clear to Jobs was that Apple could make it happen.

Some would later accuse Apple of ripping off Xerox's ideas. Jobs didn't discourage that when he often quoted Picasso as saying, "Good artists copy, great artists steal." In truth Xerox had the ideas, but it had not developed them to the point where they could be incorporated into a simple desktop computer. Jobs attributed the short-sightedness to the fact that Xerox was run by "toner heads"—sales-oriented copier executives—who "grabbed defeat from the greatest victory of the computer industry." Xerox would try later to bring its amazing work to market, but would miss the mark with a 1981 computer for the office that cost $16,595.

Meanwhile, Apple, now going up against new personal computers from much bigger companies like Texas Instruments and RadioShack, needed something special to keep its products competitive in an increasingly crowded playing field. Its Apple II was selling faster and faster, driven by Woz's clever work and an ever-greater amount of software written specifically for it—but that wouldn't last forever in such a fast-changing world.

Behind the scenes, the company was working on a computer for the office called the Apple III, which would be introduced in 1980. But it also had two other projects underway, one for a very low-cost everyman's computer, and another that would be a faster, more sophisticated machine using the latest technology. That project was called Lisa.

(For a time, Apple insisted that Lisa was an acronym for "local integrated systems architecture," meaningless but official-sounding tech gobbledygook. But as you've already figured out, it was really named for Jobs's daughter.)

Immediately, Jobs began looking for ways to incorporate the clever ideas he had seen into the Lisa computer. He contacted Dean Hovey of Hovey-Kelley Design and ordered up a mouse—though Hovey had no idea what a mouse was. Jobs explained how it should work and that it should move in all directions, not just up and down or left and right. He also made clear that he wanted to be able to use this mouse on his jeans as well as on a desktop surface.

Inspired, but unsure of the parts, Hovey headed to Walgreens. There he bought several types of roll-on deodorants to study their ball mechanisms, and a small butter dish to act as the rectangular block on top. From those, he built the first rolling-mouse prototype.

While the Xerox mouse had three buttons, Jobs insisted that the Lisa mouse have only one, so users wouldn't have to look at it as they worked. Lisa designers preferred a second button that would work something like the shift key on the keyboard. But to make one button work, they taught it two moves—the click and the now-familiar double-click.

Jobs was so energized by what he had seen at Xerox that he began to push the Lisa team to develop more new tools and graphics and to aspire to a bigger, more cosmic goal. He urged them on, saying, "Let's make a dent in the universe. We'll make it so important that it will make a dent in the universe," said Trip Hawkins, an Apple marketing manager who went on to found the gaming company Electronic Arts.

Since he didn't have a specific role to play at Apple, Jobs began to gradually take over the project.

This worried Mike Scott. The Lisa was to be an innovative product for the business market and he doubted that Jobs, who was disruptive and overbearing, could manage a division. Just recently, the Apple III had suffered partly at his hands. Unlike the Apple II, which had been designed largely by Woz, the Apple III was designed by committee, with everyone involved putting a fingerprint on it.

As he did with the Apple II, Jobs insisted on designing the case, but the one he approved for the Apple III wasn't big enough to fit all the circuitry that needed to go inside it. The engineers jerry-rigged the boards, but that created problems later. Some components simply didn't work well, and that huge catalog of Apple II software would run on the machine only if you disabled some of the newer features. New software needed to be written.

After the Apple III came out in late 1980, some chips regularly managed to wiggle loose. Until the machine could be redesigned, the company recommended lifting the front end a few inches and letting it drop. While that seemed to push chips back in their place, it was an embarrassing, low-tech solution.

Though the Apple III was a mess, improved versions of the Apple II continued to fly off the shelves. By fall 1981, the company had sold more than three hundred thousand of the beige boxes and recorded $335 million in annual sales. But the Apple III was a dud that never sold well, raising questions about Apple's ability to make a serious computer for the office.

Steve Jobs, John Sculley, and Steve Wozniak unveiling a new Apple computer.

Lisa would be another chance, and Jobs dearly wanted to run the Lisa project. But Scott put someone else in charge. In a management shuffle, Jobs was named chairman of the company, the top position, but he essentially was a figurehead who would continue to be the public face and voice of Apple. He was hurt and angry at being removed from Lisa, but it freed him to focus on the immediate task at hand: Apple was about to sell its shares to the public for the first time.

Going public, as the process is called, is a rite of passage for fast-growing companies, a way to bring in a broader swath of investors by allowing anyone to buy shares—or ownership—of a tiny bite of Apple. The money raised from selling stock to the public would fuel more growth. In addition, once stock is sold, it is traded among investors, making it easier for employees and executives to sell their stock if they want to.

But going public comes with all kinds of responsibilities; financial results and important news have to be reported so that investors can make good decisions. Executives' pay also has to be disclosed. For top managers, being in the public eye is a lot more work.

Knowing how loyal Apple users were and how successful the company had become, everyone wanted some Apple stock. Many salaried employees had been awarded shares as part of their pay. But employees who were paid by the hour were not, and that included some of the earliest and most loyal people—such as Bill Fernandez, Daniel Kottke, and Chris Espinosa.

Jobs's longtime college friend Kottke was particularly distressed and tried unsuccessfully to get Jobs to discuss the issue with him. Finally, another longtime manager urged Jobs to give Kottke some of his stock and offered to match whatever Jobs gave with some of his own.

"Great, I'll give him zero," Jobs snapped.

Wozniak, believing his shares totaled more money than he would ever need, gave stock to his parents and his brother and sister, and also gave shares to some of the old colleagues who hadn't gotten any. He also sold eighty thousand of his shares to coworkers at a price that turned out to be a nice discount to what it would be a few months later.

In addition, Wozniak's wife, Alice, had asked for a divorce, and she would end up with another chunk of his holdings.

On December 12, 1980, the stock of Apple Computer Inc. was sold in the largest public offering since Ford Motor Company sold shares in 1956. The 4.6 million shares were snapped up quickly at $22 each, but demand was so strong that the price shot up to $29 the first day. Twenty-five-year-old Steve Jobs owned 15 percent of the company, now worth close to $220 million. Despite all his other sales, Wozniak's stock was worth $116 million. At least forty other Apple employees had become millionaires. It was a heady time. The sudden wealth was exciting but also distracting and unsettling for many people at Apple.

Wozniak had continued to work on the Apple II, but was struggling to find a place in the much bigger company. He was easily distracted and would move to another project when he got bored with the last one, even if the last one wasn't finished. He found a new girlfriend and took up flying.

Not long after the public offering, he was flying with his girlfriend and two other friends on a short trip when he had trouble taking off. The plane crashed, injuring the passengers and leaving Wozniak with a missing tooth and with temporary amnesia.

After his recovery, he took a long break from the company to go back to Berkeley to finish his college degree, registering as "Rocky Raccoon Clark." He had come to realize that he didn't need much to enjoy his life, as long as he could laugh, be with family and friends, and pursue whatever he found interesting. Worrying about sales goals, the competition, and slaying corporate dragons just wasn't his thing, and it never would be. "I figure happiness is the most important thing in life, just how much you laugh," he said later. "That's who I am, who I want to be, and have always wanted to be."

For his part, Jobs gave stock worth $750,000 to his parents. They were able to pay off their mortgage for the first time and threw a little party to celebrate. They splurged each year with a cruise. But otherwise, they went about their normal lives.

Money and Apple's success made Jobs into something of a celebrity. For the next couple of years, he would grace several magazine covers as the youthful face of a generation of inventors and businessmen bringing computing to the masses.

He didn't mind the money—he certainly wasn't giving it away like Wozniak—but it wasn't his focus, and he refused to let it drive him. "The journey is the reward," he said. "It's not just the accomplishment of something incredible. It's the actual doing of something incredible, day in and day out, getting the chance to participate in something really incredible."

Before long, he would find a place for himself at Apple in the middle of just that kind of incredible experience. And it was none too soon. The giant International Business Machines, known as IBM, the most dominant computer company in the world, was about to come roaring into the personal computer business.

The dream team behind the Macintosh in 1984 (Jobs far right).

10

Pirates

When Steve Jobs spoke to the Stanford graduating class of 2005, his first story involved connecting dots between his parents' promise to his birth mother that he would go to college and his decision to drop out of Reed after one semester. Now, in 1981, at the age of twenty-six, the rest of the story was coming together.

After his exile from the Lisa project and the successful public offering, Jobs shifted his attention to a small Apple project to build a simple, inexpensive computer for everyone. The secret project, dubbed Macintosh, had nearly been killed a couple of times and was housed in a separate building, away from the main operation.

As Jobs took more interest in the idea of a simple, inexpensive computer and moved to control the project, he also began to push for some of the exciting innovations he had seen at Xerox. One of those had been a choice of wonderful fonts. Until then, computers had only one typeface, a boxy, jagged version that was easy to display on inexpensive monitors.

Jobs pushed for the Macintosh to adopt the ability to let users choose from a menu of typefaces in different sizes, in bold and italic, all proportionately spaced. To make the typefaces even more special, he insisted that they be named after world-class cities—New York, London, Geneva, and Chicago.

The decision drew on his experience at Reed College. There, because he wasn't taking required classes, he had dropped into a class on calligraphy and the elements of beautiful type-styles. At the time, the studies seemed completely random. But now, in the early 1980s, they were useful again.

Thanks in large part to that class at Reed, the Mac would be the first personal computer to give users the chance to write attractive business letters or make signs or flyers. It was an odd and unexpected chain of events: Jobs's decision to quit college and drop in on a calligraphy class led to a new use for the personal computer that would be copied by others.

He couldn't have envisioned all that when he was just seventeen. That revelation, that experience, taught him a valuable lesson, he told the Stanford graduates. Because we can't see what's ahead, "you have to trust that the dots will somehow connect in your future."

In the same way, the company reorganization and the ejection from the Lisa project—similar connecting dots—led Jobs to the Macintosh. This, too, was another bit of karma, almost like the way the very first Apple came together in the Jobs garage.

Jef Raskin, who had named the project by intentionally misspelling his favorite apple, dreamed of building an inexpensive computer as friendly and useful as a kitchen appliance, a concept that appealed to Jobs's desire to make computing available to everyone. But when Jobs began to meddle in the work, and then dictate what the computer should be, he rubbed people the wrong way.

In a blistering memo to Apple President Mike Scott in early 1981, Raskin called Jobs "a dreadful manager," noting that he regularly missed appointments, acted without thinking, and didn't give credit where it was due. He went on to spell out a criticism that would be repeated throughout Jobs's career: "Very often, when told of a new idea, he will immediately attack it and say that it is worthless or even stupid," Raskin wrote. Then, "if the idea is a good one, [Jobs] will soon be telling people about it as though it was his own."

Everything Raskin wrote may have been completely true—but it didn't go over well. He was summoned to a meeting with Jobs and when the two agreed that they couldn't agree, Raskin was asked to take a leave of absence.

Scott, too, was having his troubles. He had brought organization and structure to Apple and kept Steve Jobs in check for four years. But Scott was always a bit of a bully, and as Apple grew, he developed health problems and his management style grew erratic. In March 1981, just a few months after Apple's public offering, he summarily fired about forty employees that he decided weren't good enough. The dismissals, which came to be called Black Wednesday, upset employees and reverberated throughout the company.

Scott was pushed out soon after. Markkula became president, and Jobs now had far more freedom than he had enjoyed in some time.

Jobs quickly took charge of the Macintosh project. One of his first moves was to build a team of "A" players. Andy Hertzfeld was working on the Apple II and was eager to join the Macintosh project. He interviewed with Jobs one morning and then went back to his work. That afternoon, Jobs peered over his cubicle and told him he had the job.

"Hey, that's great," Hertzfeld said. He would just need a day or two to finish what he was working on.

Jobs had a different idea. "What's more important than working on the Macintosh?" he asked.

"With that," Hertzfeld recalled later, "he walked over to my desk, found the power cord to my Apple II, gave it a sharp tug, and pulled it out of the socket." Everything Hertzfeld had been working on was gone. Jobs stacked the monitor on top of the computer and told Hertzfeld, "Come with me. I'm going to take you to your new desk."

The new desk turned out to be Raskin's old one.

Over the next three years, the small group in the project

witnessed the best and worst of Jobs—his charm and his cutting criticisms, his exuberance and arrogance, and his vision, his ability to look at something very ordinary and intuitively see the potential for it to become something truly extraordinary. He didn't want a good product, or even a great one. The Macintosh, he would say over and over, had to be "insanely great."

While driven to do better and better work, as defined by Jobs, the members of the team tried to adjust to their boss's erratic ways. Jobs would take a look at someone's work and declare it a pile of garbage, often using stronger language. Or he might say, " 'This is the greatest thing I've ever seen,' " Hertzfeld said. "The scary thing was that he'd say it about the same thing."

Bud Tribble, another member of the team, defined a unique Jobs trait that the Mac team—or any other team that Jobs worked with—could never figure out how to turn off. Tribble dubbed it Jobs's "reality distortion field," a term he took from the *Star Trek* television series. "In his presence, reality is malleable," he explained. "He can convince anyone of practically anything. It wears off when he's not around."

At various points, Jobs's reality distortion field would lead him to act as if the rules of life didn't apply to him. He drove his car without a license plate and regularly parked in Apple's handicapped spots. He would quote totally made-up statements as fact, expect results on unrealistic schedules, or set impossibly high goals. People would believe him when he was around and only come to their senses after he left. But because he pushed so hard, sometimes they made the impossible come true.

Jobs sweated every detail of the Macintosh. He obsessed over the title bars, as the headings at the top of each screen and document were called, insisting the designers redo them again and again—more than a dozen times. When the designers protested, he shot back, "Can you imagine looking at that every day? It's not just a little thing."

At one point, he wanted to change the name of the Macintosh to "Bicycle," because, just as a bicycle improved a human's speed, the computer would act as a "bicycle for the mind." The team had to talk him out of it.

One software designer, who was writing a drawing program that would come with the computer, found a way to create ovals and circles quickly. Jobs liked it, but immediately wanted something else: Could it also create rectangles with rounded corners?

The designer balked, adding that would be tough and wasn't really necessary.

But Jobs wouldn't hear of it. "Rectangles with rounded corners are everywhere!" he insisted, and he began to call out examples around the room. Then he dragged the designer on a walk around the block, pointing out a NO PARKING sign with rounded corners. On seeing this, the designer gave in and added "RoundRects" to his repertoire.

Sometimes, the designers pushed back—but not too hard. Chris Espinosa, who had started in the Jobs's garage, got tired of Jobs's endless tinkering of his design of a little calculator that would be part of the computer's desktop. Each time he saw it, Jobs would disapprove: The lines were too thick, the background too dark, or the buttons were the wrong size.

Finally, Espinosa created a little program he called "The Steve Jobs Roll-Your-Own Calculator Construction Set," allowing Jobs to adjust all of the variables himself. Jobs sat down and fiddled for a little while, finally settling on his choices. That design would be the Macintosh calculator for many years.

As the work moved forward, Jobs worried that the little computer took too long to boot up. He urged the team to cut the time with a little reality-distorting math. Guessing that within a few years five million people a day would be using a Mac—a ridiculous estimate given that only a few hundred thousand Apple IIs had been sold over several years—he noted that slashing ten seconds would save fifty million seconds every day. "Over a year, that's probably dozens of lifetimes," he told them. Now on a roll, he made a particularly big leap: "If you could make it boot ten seconds faster, you'll save a dozen lives. That's really worth it, don't you think?"

The team figured out how to shorten the boot-up time.

In every case, he was seeking something that would be easier and simpler to use because, as the original brochure said, "Simplicity is the ultimate sophistication." When you first look at a problem, it seems easy because you don't know that much about it, he said. Then, "you get into the problem and you see it's really complicated and you come up with all these convoluted solutions."

Most people stop there. But the key is to keep going, he said, until you find the "underlying principle of the problem and sort of come full circle with a beautiful, elegant solution that works." Perhaps drawing on his Zen studies, Jobs focused as intensely on what to leave out of a product as on what to put in.

He lavished special attention on the look of the Mac. Again Jobs studied household appliances, especially the Cuisinart. Instead of a rectangular box, the computer was made taller and thinner, so it would take up less desk space. In contrast to the Apple II, the keyboard was detached.

The initial versions were too boxy for Jobs's taste. "It's got to be more curvaceous," he urged. Finally, when he approved the design, he asked key members of the team to sign their names to the mold. In a special touch, their signatures were imprinted inside the case. Though no one but technicians would ever see them, the artists had signed their most significant work.

The new computer would have a new kind of floppy disk drive, which used three-and-a-half-inch disks encased in hard plastic—small enough to fit in a shirt pocket—instead of the flimsy, bigger ones. (Though rarely used now, these square disks are the "save" icon in most computer programs.) But at the same time, Jobs pushed through questionable decisions over team objections. To force buyers to use the mouse, he took arrow keys that move the cursor off the keyboard. Though hard-disk drives installed inside the computer had much more storage than floppy disk drives and were becoming common, he refused to put one in the Mac because he didn't want to add a noisy fan to keep it cool. And he agreed to a design with only 128 kilobytes (or 128,000 bytes) of memory—a slender amount for a machine with so much detail on the screen. By contrast, the Lisa was designed with ten times more memory. Ignoring the lesson Wozniak had tried to teach him by including expansion slots for the Apple II, Jobs made the Macintosh so difficult to open up that only determined tech geeks could figure out how to add more memory.

While relentlessly driving the team, Jobs also gave them the impression they were the hardest workers at Apple. He kept the refrigerator stocked with expensive fruit juice and paid for massages for tired engineers. Other teams came to see the group as arrogant and spoiled.

Still, as the Macintosh came closer to reality, Apple needed it to succeed more than ever. Though the various

Apple IIs didn't get much glory inside Apple, they were still carrying the company. Thanks to both Markkula and Jobs, the computer had made big inroads in schools and with college students, introducing computing to America's young. But the industry was changing fast.

In 1981, the giant International Business Machines finally entered the desktop computer business with its Personal Computer, or PC. Apple was so arrogantly confident that it was the stronger player that it bought a full-page ad in the *Wall Street Journal* that read, "Welcome IBM. Seriously. Welcome to the most exciting and important marketplace since the computer revolution began 35 years ago . . ."

Because Apple had such a head start and because there was nothing special or even fun about the IBM PC, the young Apple crew scoffed at it. But in looking only at the machine, they ignored IBM's stellar reputation, its powerful sales force, and the enormous clout it carried among business buyers. They didn't understand that a corporate technology manager might get in hot water for buying a no-name machine, but no one would ever be fired for buying an IBM.

True, the computer wasn't great. But it was good enough, and IBM's sales grew quickly as it picked up more and more business customers.

To ensure that the Mac would have software, Jobs traveled in 1981 to Seattle to meet with Bill Gates and Paul Allen, the young founders of software company Microsoft. Years earlier, Microsoft had written the first BASIC program for the Altair, and it had also written the version of BASIC now running on the Apple II. It created the operating system for the IBM computer, the software that told the computer hardware what to do and that created a basis for everything else.

Jobs set up the meeting with the hope of convincing Microsoft to do something different: He wanted the company to create a spreadsheet program for the Mac that would make it useful to businesses, much like VisiCalc had given a boost to the Apple II. In their meeting, he and Gates also shared wildly different views of where the personal computer business was going.

To Jobs, the desktop computer was for intellectuals and college students, for home users, and some mix of middle managers and secretaries. Each machine needed to be a special and amazing tool to improve their lives. But Gates saw something much bigger and much less personal. To him, the computer was a tool to help businesses run better. He saw networks of computers working together to help businesses communicate, calculate, and sell. Over the next few years, Gates's vision would be the more accurate one—but Jobs's vision was the one that prevailed at Apple.

IBM's entrance into the business, as well as the addition of more software and bigger memories and speedier processors, spurred interest in computers. Rather than single out a person as Man of the Year, *Time* magazine named the personal computer Machine of the Year for 1982. But it profiled only one person as the voice and face of the revolution: Steve Jobs. "With his smooth sales pitch and a blind faith," the magazine said, "it is Steven Jobs, more than anyone, who kicked open the door and let the personal computer move in."

For the fiscal year that ended in September 1982, Apple sold a record seven hundred thousand Apple IIs, and despite its problems with the Apple III, it reached $583 million in sales, enough to make the Fortune 500 list of America's largest companies for the first time—as Markkula had predicted years before.

But good times wouldn't last. Within two years, IBM was selling more computers than Apple, and software companies were churning out far more programs for the IBM PC than for Apple. Other computer makers rushed to license the Microsoft operating system so they could run all that new IBM software. Before long, most desktop computers were singing the same song—that is, running the same software as the IBM computer. Those that didn't, like Apple, faced an uncertain future.

The Lisa computer, which had cost about $50 million to create, was introduced in 1983 to much fanfare. It was the first computer to use a mouse, the first to offer the menus and file system that had made the Xerox visit so amazing. It was loaded with memory and two floppy drives, as well as a few easy-to-use programs that came with it. While most software at the time might take days to learn, Lisa's could be mastered in a couple of hours. But all the extras had bloated the price to $10,000, and there was no other software available. The tech crowd was wowed—but most potential customers couldn't begin to justify the steep price.

While Jobs promoted the new machine to the press, he couldn't resist dropping hints about the Macintosh. Interest in Lisa began to cool before it was ever available, since people knew a computer with similar abilities was coming out for much less money. To make matters worse, software for the Lisa wouldn't work on the Macintosh. In addition to competing with IBM, one Apple division seemed to be battling the other.

They were also battling Microsoft. In late 1983, before the Mac would be formally introduced, Microsoft announced it would create an operating system for IBM and its copycats called Windows that would incorporate icons, windows, and a mouse—just like the Mac. Gates had promised to wait a year after the Mac shipping date before selling so-called graphical interfaces. But because the Mac had slipped almost a year behind schedule, Microsoft was catching up.

Jobs was livid and summoned Gates to Apple's Cupertino headquarters to yell at him in front of Apple managers.

But Gates couldn't be rattled. "Well, Steve, I think there's more than one way of looking at it," he told Jobs and others in the conference room. "I think it's more like we both had this rich neighbor named Xerox and I broke into his house to steal the TV set and found that you had already stolen it."

It would actually take Microsoft many years to truly compete with Apple, though that didn't calm Jobs down. Jobs still believed his baby alone would lead a computer revolution. At a retreat the month that Lisa was launched, he implored the Mac team to work even harder with a few pithy slogans. "Real Artists Ship," he told them, meaning they could no longer let deadlines slip but had to get their product out. And, he wrote, "It's better to be a pirate than join the Navy," implying that his rebellious group's technology was much better than what everyone else was offering.

The team was inspired. A couple of them created a pirate flag, with a skull, crossbones, and the colorful Apple logo for an eye patch, and flew it from the Macintosh building. They had given it their all. But would they really end up with the loot?

Apples for the Teacher

From almost the beginning of the company, Apple helped bring computers into schools.

When Mike Markkula's daughter was in grade school in 1978, he began to believe a computer could help her learn math. Inspired by that belief, the Apple Education Foundation was formed to give money and computers to teachers and others who wanted to write educational software.

It was a clever move; more educational software was available for the Apple II computers, more schools bought them than other brands, and many young people got their first introduction to computing on an Apple. Then, because kids were familiar with the computers at school, they asked their parents to buy them.

In the early 1980s, Steve Jobs tried to convince Congress to pass a bill to allow Apple to donate one hundred thousand computers to schools in exchange for a tax deduction. Jobs called it the Kids Can't Wait law, but it never got out of the Senate. California, however, got on board and Apple ended up donating about ten thousand computers to the state's schools.

The company tried to build the same kind of brand loyalty between Macintosh and college students, urging universities to commit millions of dollars to bring personal computing to their programs. Again, as a result, Apple's computers were the top choice on campus.

Even today, Apple gives a discount to college students who buy its computers. And in 2011, it arranged for the nine thousand college graduates who are part of Teach for America to each receive a refurbished iPad.

John Sculley (right) with Steve Jobs in 1984, the year before their falling-out.

11

Sculley

Thanks to the unstoppable popularity of the Apple II, Apple's sales were still growing. But there was a joke that was popular in Silicon Valley: What's the difference between Apple and the Boy Scouts?

The answer: The Boy Scouts have adult supervision.

After Mike Scott left, Apple was in need of a true leader, someone who could channel Jobs's energy and passion and put all the company's youthful creativity and intelligence to good use. In 1982, that search took Jobs and Mike Markkula to John Sculley, the energetic leader of Pepsi-Cola. With clever marketing and a Pepsi Challenge ad campaign, Sculley had gotten national attention, especially after Pepsi's supermarket sales briefly passed those of Coke. He was a marketing man who knew how to sell to a younger generation.

Jobs courted Sculley for months, meeting with him in

New York and also when Sculley visited in California. Sculley didn't know much about Apple initially. But on a trip to Los Angeles to see his seventeen-year-old son and nineteen-year-old daughter, he quickly learned he was dealing with a hot company. He asked his kids to go with him to a computer store and he mentioned he was about to meet Steve Jobs of Apple. Though his teens went to school with children of celebrities, they responded as if he were about to meet a major rock star.

"Steve Jobs?" his daughter said. "You're going to meet Steve Jobs?"

Over and over during the visits, Sculley insisted he was happy in his job and loved the East Coast, where Pepsi was based. But once Jobs decided Sculley was his man, he turned on the full force of his charm. Finally, after a long visit one day in New York, Jobs issued the challenge that changed Sculley's mind: "Do you want to spend the rest of your life selling sugared water or do you want a chance to change the world?"

At forty-four years old, Sculley joined Apple in the spring of 1983, with a $1 million paycheck and the promise of a $1 million bonus.

Initially, he and Jobs got along beautifully, talking several times a day, taking long walks, and even finishing each other's sentences. They were so close that over breakfast one day at Jobs's house, Jobs told Sculley and his wife why he was in such a hurry. "We all have a short period of time on this earth," Jobs said. "We probably only have the opportunity to do a few things really great and do them really well. . . . My feeling is I've got to accomplish a lot of these things while I'm young."

In Jobs's enthusiasm and commitment, Sculley saw his younger self. "I was fascinated by his mind and vision and my place in it. I could help Steve become the Henry Ford of the computer age."

Jobs had several heroes, including Edwin Land, founder of Polaroid; inventor Thomas Edison; and Henry Ford, who had taken an expensive product—the car—and adopted more efficient manufacturing methods so he could sell it to the masses at an affordable price. Jobs wanted a computer for the masses as well, one that was designed for the user, not for the geeks in corporate tech departments.

To fulfill that dream, he wanted to price the Macintosh at $2,000. But he also wanted a huge advertising budget. Sculley told him he couldn't have it both ways; if he was going to spend so much on marketing, it had to be factored into the price. He finally convinced Jobs that the Macintosh would have to sell at $2,495, a price Jobs thought was too high.

Despite that disagreement, Sculley got behind the massive publicity campaign to launch the new computer. A special television commercial was commissioned that was as strange and quirky as any ever seen. Both men loved it, but when they showed it to the Apple board of directors, every one of them hated it. The company had paid $750,000 for the ad, filmed by *Blade Runner* director Ridley Scott, and was committed to spend about $800,000 to air it during the Super Bowl. Now that looked like a foolish thing to do.

The pair asked the agency to sell the time to someone else. But when the agency came back to say it couldn't get a good price, Apple decided to go with the commercial.

During the third quarter of the Los Angeles Raiders' thumping of the Washington Redskins on Super Bowl Sunday, television screens across America went dark before rows of bald men in baggy clothing marched monotonously into a room and sat on wooden benches. With blank faces, they watched a screen, where a *Wizard of Oz*–like Big Brother was lecturing them (a not-very-subtle reference to IBM). The camera cut to a blond woman, wearing red shorts and a Macintosh T-shirt running into the room carrying a sledgehammer. Suddenly, she stopped, swung the hammer, and sent it hurling into the screen, which exploded in bright light.

"On January 24, Apple Computer will introduce Macintosh," a narrator says. Then, making a reference to the George Orwell classic, he adds, "You'll see why 1984 won't be like *1984.*"

The ad was creepy, odd, and completely mesmerizing. And to many of the nearly one hundred million people who saw it, it was the best part of the football game.

A few days later, Jobs made a formal introduction to Apple shareholders at the annual meeting. Presenting the new machine as part of a showdown between Apple and IBM, he rallied the crowd by showing

Apple's "1984" Super Bowl ad featured a woman wearing the Apple logo running through ranks of baggy-clothed businessmen to smash a large screen with the face of Big Brother on it. The ad won four different awards and is widely regarded as one of the best commercials of all time.

the commercial again. Then, like the showman he had become, he pulled a Macintosh out of a bag by the small handle on the top, described its special features, and pulled a little floppy from his shirt pocket. Running the disk, the Mac began to show off its skills—its fonts, charts, games, and drawings. Finally, Jobs pressed a button on the mouse, and in a computer voice, the computer began to talk: "Hello, I'm Macintosh. It sure is great to get out of that bag. . . ."

The crowd went wild.

Over the next few weeks, Jobs would deliver Macintoshes himself to Mick Jagger (actually leaving it with his daughter), and to Sean Lennon, the young son of Yoko Ono and the late John Lennon, among other celebrities. Dozens of

Steve Jobs posing with his beloved Macintosh in his home in 1984.

reporters had been given advanced briefings and they filled magazines and newspapers with glowing reviews. The machine flew off the shelves, selling about seventy thousand in one hundred days, more than the initial sales of the IBM PC.

The frenzy didn't last long. After the early rush, sales began to slide. Over Christmas 1985, Apple had expected to sell about 150,000 machines, but sold only about a hundred thousand. Then sales fell further.

All of the limitations that Jobs had imposed—the crummy memory and the lack of expansion slots, cursors keys, and a hard drive—were discouraging new buyers. The minimal memory was a particular problem. One Apple insider compared it to trying to run a Honda on a one-gallon gas tank. Because so much of the computer's memory was needed to sustain the activities on the screen, the word-processing program couldn't handle more than eight pages at a time, hardly enough to pen a chapter. Because it tended to overheat, some critics called the Mac a "beige toaster."

Worse, in early 1985, Apple bombed with another costly Super Bowl commercial in which corporate personal computer users were portrayed as "lemmings," following one another off a cliff. The ad was seen as an insult to the people who bought most personal computers and it left a sour taste behind.

In early 1985, Jobs turned thirty, throwing a fancy dinner dance for three hundred people, with singer Ella Fitzgerald as the entertainment. His guests brought him special presents—fine wine, crystal, a first-edition book, and even a framed share of IBM stock—but he left them all in a hotel room. He wasn't much interested in those material things.

Around that time, he sat down for a long magazine interview. Apple's stock, which had peaked at about $63.50 a share during the Lisa excitement in mid-1983, had sunk, and the value of Jobs's stock had fallen more than $200 million from a peak above $450 million. He laughed at the enormous loss, saying, "It's hardly the most insightful or valuable thing that's happened to me in the past ten years."

He had been thinking about an old Hindu saying: "For the first thirty years of your life, you make your habits. For the last thirty years of your life, your habits make you." And he was reflective about Apple, almost predicting that major changes were ahead: "I hope that throughout my life I'll sort of have the thread of my life and the thread of Apple weave in and out of each other, like a tapestry. There may be a few years when I'm not there, but I'll always come back."

His old friend Steve Wozniak had done that—after getting his degree, he had returned to Apple in 1983 to work on improvements to the Apple II. But in February 1985, he left again, saying he wanted to develop a new kind of remote control. He was also upset that the company he cofounded was mostly ignoring the Apple II, repeatedly focusing on the newest computers in the family when the various Apple IIs provided most of its sales. Woz also revealed that he had sold most of his stock, putting $70 million into safe investments.

Still, he wasn't leaving completely; he would remain a consultant on a modest retainer, reported at $12,000, and would remain a public face of Apple.

In March 1985, President Ronald Reagan honored Jobs and Wozniak, along with a few others, with the first National Medal of Technology and Innovation. Because Wozniak had just left the company, Apple didn't send a delegation or plan a celebration. The two simply stopped at a sandwich shop after the ceremony.

Sculley also had his hands full. Apple couldn't afford for the Mac to fail—a third strike after the Apple III fiasco and a poor showing by Lisa, which sold less than half of what was expected.

Amid the turmoil, Jobs and Sculley began to bicker and blame each other. Sculley realized that he, too, had been caught in Jobs's reality distortion field. He concluded Jobs was meddling too much in other operations, giving too many orders, changing plans, and not delivering the Macintosh changes that were sorely needed. Jobs questioned Sculley's ability and whether he really understood technology or the computer business.

At a meeting of the board of directors in April 1985,

longtime directors called Sculley on the carpet. He had been hired as the chief executive officer—and he needed to take the reins, not share them with Jobs. Saying Jobs had been "acting like a petulant brat," they made it clear Jobs would be replaced as the head of the newly combined Mac and Lisa division by someone with more experience. The board, including Mike Markkula, gave Sculley the freedom to make the changes when he was ready.

Throughout his childhood, his teen years, and his adult life to date, Jobs wasn't able to accept the word "no"—and he still couldn't. He lobbied Sculley for a reprieve. He cried. He railed and felt betrayed. Calling Sculley a "bozo"—a favorite word for describing someone he thought was an idiot or fool—he even tried to pull off a coup by rallying other executives and board members to oust Sculley. None of that worked.

For a time, Sculley tried to convince him to lead an Apple research and development effort, but Jobs rejected that idea. In early summer, Sculley removed Jobs as the head of the Macintosh division, saying his new role would be "global visionary." Jobs's office was moved to a building that had been largely vacated; Jobs called it "Siberia."

A month later, Sculley told Wall Street analysts, "From an operations standpoint, there is no role either today or in the future for Steve Jobs." He added, "I don't know what he'll do. I don't think he knows. Only time and Steve Jobs will tell."

Jobs was deeply hurt and felt like he had been punched in the stomach so hard that he couldn't breathe. Apple had been just about the only focus of his adult life. The more he tried to catch his breath, the harder it got. "If I tried to figure out what to do or sort out my life or all that stuff, it was just like trying to breathe harder," he said. For much of the summer, Jobs traveled, going to Europe and Russia as an Apple emissary, and even briefly considered staying in Europe as an expatriate artist.

He also considered going into politics, but he had never actually voted, which would have been a drawback.

He was thirty years old, a millionaire, and a failure at the company he cofounded. He didn't know what to do.

Heroes

Steve Jobs had several heroes, starting with the brilliant scientist Albert Einstein, whose picture hung in Jobs's largely unfurnished bedroom.

Jobs also had huge respect for Akio Morita, cofounder of Sony, the giant consumer electronics company, who set high standards and truly appreciated beauty. When Morita died in 1999, Jobs paid him his highest possible compliment during a presentation, saying, "He expressed his love for the human species in every product he made."

Then there was Edwin Land, a Harvard dropout who built Polaroid Corporation after inventing a camera system capable of taking and developing photos almost instantly. Jobs called him "a national treasure."

In 1980, Land was pushed out of Polaroid after an attempt at making an instant movie system couldn't compete with videotape recording. The company had to write off its large investment. That distressed Jobs. "All he did was blow a lousy few million and they took his company away from him," he said.

A few years after that, Sculley and Jobs met with Land at his Cambridge lab and Land explained his invention: "I could see what the Polaroid camera should be. It was just as real to me as if it was sitting in front of me before I had ever built one."

That hit home with Jobs. "That's exactly the way I saw the Macintosh," he said. "There was no way to do consumer research on it, so I had to go and create it and then show it to people."

Even more impressive to Jobs, Land was both an artist and a scientist. Land wanted his company "to stand at the intersection of art and science, and I've never forgotten that," Jobs said.

Part 2

"Real artists ship."

12

Next

Steve Jobs's first story for the 2005 Stanford graduating class was about connecting dots—or letting the dots connect for you.

His second story, he said, "is about love and loss."

Recounting how he and Wozniak started Apple in the Jobs garage, he said, "I was lucky—I found what I loved to do early in life." He had the joy of helping Apple grow to almost $2 billion in sales, with more than four thousand employees, in ten years. The Macintosh had made a huge splash in the computer world just as technology's boy wonder had turned thirty.

Then, he said, "I got fired."

It was a bone-rattling experience. He explained that he had hired a talented executive, but after a year "our visions of the future began to diverge and eventually we had a falling out." (This was a more-generous-than-usual retelling. More

Opposite page: After leaving Apple, Jobs formed a new computer company called NeXT.

commonly, he pinned all the problems on Sculley, saying in 1995, "I hired the wrong guy, and he destroyed everything I'd spent ten years working for.")

Without Apple, Jobs was shaken and devastated, unsure what to do next. But then, he said, "Something slowly began to dawn on me: I still loved what I did."

Even without Apple, he could pursue his vision and his passion. He could still try to create another great product. So, he decided to start another company.

In truth, Jobs didn't handle the starting-over part very well. He was still the chairman of Apple when he concluded there might be a market for very powerful machines for universities, especially for scientists who needed to be able to run simulations for research. He decided to start a new company.

Initially Apple's board was open to him starting a new company and even considered making an investment. But within days, the board members learned Jobs had lined up five key engineers and salespeople who would follow him out the door. Their response turned to anger, and they felt deceived.

Amid the tumult, Jobs resigned in September 1985, saying in a letter, "The company's recent reorganization left me with no work to do and no access even to regular management reports. I am but thirty and want still to contribute and achieve."

Apple responded by suing Jobs, charging that he was taking trade secrets with him. (The suit would be settled in a few months, with Jobs agreeing to focus on a different market from Apple's.)

Jobs responded by selling his nearly 10 percent ownership of Apple over several months. Though the stock was trading at a depressed $18 a share, well below the all-time peak above $60, he cleared well over $100 million. He kept one share—so he could still go to shareholder meetings.

In 1987, Apple would turn around, thanks to seeds that Jobs had planted. Just as VisiCalc had given Apple II meaning, new software, a memory upgrade, and the laser printer introduced before Jobs left would highlight Mac's fonts and other skills, making the computer a wizard at desktop publishing. Suddenly, newsletter writers, company public relations offices, graphic artists, and even PTA moms could create their professional-looking documents and presentations at their own desks. The business, along with the Mac's appeal to individuals, would open up a big enough niche for Apple to continue to expand for some years, even as IBM computers and their look-alikes took over more and more of an exploding personal computer market. By 1993, Apple's sales would grow to $8 billion in sales under Sculley.

Cut loose from Apple, Jobs put his money on two companies in 1986. He initially invested $7 million in the new computer company that he formed, named Next. And he spent $5 million to buy a small maker of computer graphics equipment called Pixar from *Star Wars* filmmaker George Lucas, agreeing to invest another $5 million into the business.

Like Jobs, both companies would struggle for the next few years to find their place in the universe.

This time, there was no adult supervision. Without someone like Mike Markkula or John Sculley watching at Next, Jobs was free to do whatever he wanted, whenever. One of his first steps was to create the perfect logo. After four designers didn't measure up, Jobs agreed to pay the outrageous sum of $100,000 to Paul Rand, who had designed the ABC television and IBM logos. Rand told him he would get only one logo—and no others. Because Jobs planned on building a computer shaped like a cube, Rand offered up a cube logo with colorful type, including a lowercase *e*, which he told Jobs could mean "education, excellence, expertise, exceptional, excitement, $e = mc^2$."

Jobs loved it. From then on, the company would be known as NeXT.

For the time being, at least, Jobs had discovered what gave his life meaning, and it was work—"not just work, but nonstop work, no-other-life work," wrote journalist Joe Nocera in a 1986 *Esquire* profile. "You have to have a real single-minded tunnel vision if you want to get anything significant accomplished," Jobs said, adding that he believed he has more great products in him. "If I can create the kind of company I think we can, it will give me an *extreme* amount of pleasure."

NeXT would get a boost the following year when Texas computer billionaire H. Ross Perot saw a PBS television show featuring Jobs and called the younger man about investing in the new venture. Though Jobs's own money was running low and he was desperate for an investment, he played it cool. Perot ended up paying $20 million for about 16 percent of the upstart. Jobs put in another $5 million and Stanford and Carnegie Mellon universities got together to buy 1 percent of the company.

As he had at Apple, Jobs obsessed over many details. This time, he was on a special mission: "Part of Steve wanted to prove to others and to himself that Apple wasn't just luck," said Andrea Cunningham, who had been a publicist for NeXT.

He insisted on a cube design, even though that didn't make a lot of sense for circuit boards. He wanted the computer to have a stunning black finish, even on the inside. When a tiny line appeared on the box, he traveled to Chicago to discuss it with the die caster that made it. Even the factory had to be perfect, with white walls and machines painted in his choice of colors. An elegant, custom staircase, much like the one often seen in Apple retail stores today, graced both the factory and the specially designed corporate headquarters.

As he was at Apple, Jobs was often intimidating and demanding, quick to yell at his designers or engineers or sharply criticize their work. Employees told *The New York Times* about the "three times" rule: The first time Jobs heard an idea he didn't like, he "berates the offending employee, calling the idea or product brain-damaged." The second time, he liked it better—and "the third time he will call it insanely great."

Though he had promised the machine would cost about $3,000, near the high end of what students and universities might pay, the price began to swell as he added optical disks that could write and rewrite, sort of like CD burners today; tons of memory and data storage, and other features. The computer would also feature unique software that would make programming like building with LEGOS, much simpler than having to create everything from scratch.

He had never been one to ask customers what they preferred. One of his idols, car maker Henry Ford, once famously said that customers could have their Model Ts in any color they wanted—as long as it was black. In this case, Jobs never nailed down who would really want (or use) these high-powered machines in the first place.

The computer was initially supposed to be out in 1987, but the deadline slipped and slipped again. In Silicon Valley, wags joked that the name NeXT would be changed to "Eventually."

Finally, in October 1988, the computer was officially announced in a glitzy unveiling before three thousand educators, software developers, friends, and reporters at San Francisco's Symphony Hall. Jobs demonstrated the machine's slick graphics, an enormous memory that included the complete works of Shakespeare already installed, and the ability to play music. A Bach duet between the computer and a concert violinist ended the show.

When a reporter asked about the machine being late, Jobs didn't miss a beat. It wasn't "late," he said. It was "five years ahead of its time."

But just like with the Macintosh, there were notable flaws. The computer now cost $6,500, but with a laser printer and other necessary extras, its price was really closer to $10,000, too expensive for many buyers. The software to run the machines wasn't ready yet and wouldn't be for a few months. In addition, the computer wasn't compatible with software already on the market, so very little extra software would be available. The screen was only black and white, not color, and Jobs refused to install a floppy drive in the beautiful box, which would have made it easier for users to share data.

At one point, his staff actually revolted over that decision. When an employee questioned the lack of a floppy drive during a meeting, Jobs insisted the computer didn't need it. But another employee argued with him, and everyone in the meeting broke into a strongly worded chant: "We need a ———— floppy; We need a ———— floppy!"

Jobs agreed only to include a floppy drive on a later model.

Still, the Japanese company Canon was impressed enough to invest $100 million in 1989 for a 16.7 percent piece of the company, giving NeXT important cash while it tried to roll out its computers. By then, however, much had changed in the dozen years since the Apple II was introduced. While all the players in the early days were newcomers scrambling for attention, there were now plenty of major computer makers with deep pockets that would give computers to educators to entice them to buy more. As a startup, NeXT had significant competition.

Even though NeXT had yet to take off, *Inc.* magazine in 1989 named Jobs "Entrepreneur of the Decade" for his role in starting and shaping the personal computer revolution. But his special touch wouldn't extend to the new computer. Despite all the care and attention Jobs showered on the company, NeXT would ship only about a thousand test computers in 1989. Time and again, Jobs would announce that NeXT was bringing the world a breakthrough. But the customers didn't follow and NeXT wasn't close to making a profit, which companies must do to thrive and grow.

At a board meeting in spring 1991, company officials delivered more bad news about poor results. Investor Ross Perot interrupted the presentation with a blunt assessment: "So what you're telling me is the cockpit's on fire and the plane's in a tailspin. So tell me something that I don't know."

NeXT was barely puttering along—though customers found NeXT's software remarkable. As the new decade started, customers told Jobs over and over to ditch the computer and sell his programs instead. But having grown up as a computer maker, he ignored their recommendations. He couldn't bear to give up the machines.

Still, by 1992, only about fifty thousand NeXT computers had been sold in total—about what Apple was now selling in a week.

Pixar wasn't faring much better.

Director George Lucas, who was in the midst of a divorce, initially wanted a much higher price for the business, but settled for Jobs's fire-sale offer after other possible buyers fell through. The potential captured Jobs's imagination.

Thanks to films like *Star Wars*, movie makers were trying much more sophisticated special effects—but doing them without computers was about as difficult as becoming a Jedi Knight. In some instances, Lucas had to cobble together thirteen different pieces of film for each frame, Jobs explained in an interview. Background paintings might account for a few pieces, fixed models might account for more, and then the live action and special effects had to be added on top of those. Every time one frame was combined with another, the new image picked up noise or blurriness or other imperfections. If you stopped on a single frame of an old Star Wars movie, Jobs said, you'd see "they are really grungy. Incredibly noisy, very bad quality."

Combining the images digitally would make the frames sparkle, but there weren't computers powerful enough to do that. Pixar, made up of computer experts who loved animation, had created a sophisticated $125,000 computer that could help, and had hoped to not only begin to create great animated movies, but also find new applications in three-dimensional medical imaging, detailed mapmaking, or other fields.

Over several years, Jobs let the company run up an estimated $50 million in debts, which he personally guaranteed. But he never could find computer magic.

While he put most of his attention on NeXT, Jobs let the Pixar executives run the company. But he met regularly with them and made the key financial decisions. (The folks at NeXT sneeringly called Pixar "the hobby.")

To get sales moving, he opened Pixar sales offices in several cities. Though the price of the computer came down to less than $50,000 and an even cheaper model was developed, buyers just weren't interested. The biggest customer was the Walt Disney Company, which found it could cuts costs and speed up production of its animated movies by scanning in hand-drawn images and using the computers to add color and layers of background drawings. The first test was in the closing scene of *The Little Mermaid*. After that, Disney bought several dozen computers, using them for *The Rescuers Down Under, Beauty and the Beast,* and *The Lion King,* among others.

While the computers were a breakthrough for Disney, other heavy-duty, general purpose workstations were coming along that would eventually do the same things if equipped with the right software. Realizing the computers simply weren't selling, Jobs closed the sales offices and in 1990, he sold Pixar's computer hardware business.

Next, he tried to develop Pixar's clever 3-D software into something for a broader market, which would allow users to make realistic, three-dimensional images. But the software was never easy to use, even for the experts, and there wasn't huge demand for the idea. He shut that effort down in 1991, and let go of thirty of the company's seventy-two employees, including Pixar's president. In a particularly cold-hearted move, he refused to give the employees two weeks' notice or pay them severance, sending them home on the spot without any additional pay.

There was only one possible Pixar business left: animation. The company had been created by people who always loved cartoons and who dearly wanted to make full-length animated movies on computers. Before Jobs bought the company, the founders, Ed Catmull and Alvy Ray Smith, had snapped up John Lasseter, a talented young animator who had been let go by Disney. To show the power of the Pixar computers and software, Lasseter had created eye-popping and entertaining small movies—a short called *Luxo Jr.* featured an animated desk lamp and was nominated for an Academy Award, and *Tin Toy,* released in 1988, which won the Oscar for animated short films.

On several occasions, Jobs came close to killing

the animation business, too, but Catmull talked him out of it. Finally, Pixar found a way to make some money. It began making fun animated commercials for Listerine mouthwash, Life Savers candy, and Trident gum. After Jobs killed the software project, the commercials and the remaining professional software were about all Pixar had going for it, and that didn't add up to very much.

To keep the business afloat, Jobs struck a hard bargain with his Pixar executives and employees in 1991. He would keep funding the company, but only if they gave up any stock they owned in Pixar and any options to buy stock in the future, sacrificing their one chance to make a windfall from all their hard work over the years.

As the majority owner, Jobs could make the rules. The managers and employees gave up their small share of the company.

In fairness, said Alvy Ray Smith later, Pixar, like NeXT, "should have failed. But it seemed to me that Steve just would not suffer a defeat."

There was one ray of hope. Giant Walt Disney Company had taken notice of John Lasseter's work. It was interested in funding a full-length animated feature film that Pixar would make. Lasseter had just the idea in mind: a story about toys that yearned for kids to play with them. Appropriately, he called it *Toy Story*. In the wreckage of two failing companies, could there possibly be a happy ending?

Thank NeXT for the World Wide Web

Tim Berners-Lee was a thirty-five-year-old physicist working at CERN, the European Particle Physics Laboratory in Geneva, Switzerland, when his NeXT computer arrived in 1990 for a special project.

The result: the World Wide Web, what we know today as the Internet.

Berners-Lee asked the lab for about $50,000 in equipment and a few programmers to see if he could link together ideas and computers and make the software accessible for free. Using the NeXT computer, he put together a coding system called HTML, for HyperText Markup Language, which uses tags that allow pages to be viewed correctly. He gave each Web page a unique address, or URL, for Universal Resource Locater. He then created the rules that allowed the information to be transferred and shared, called HTTP, or HyperText Transfer Protocol. And he produced the first browser to allow users to see the results the same way.

All of this was done on a NeXT computer that came with a ready-to-use e-mail account and an audio welcome from Steve Jobs, who said the computer wasn't about personal computing, but about "'interpersonal' computing."

Berners-Lee said that the software that came with the NeXT machine made his programming work "remarkably easy." He started the work in October 1990, made it available in his lab in December, and gave it to the world in the summer of 1991. For the next couple of years, he refined it. Within about five years, the Web had forty million users.

Steve Jobs with his daughter Lisa Brennan Jobs.

13

Family

The marriage of one of high tech's most eligible bachelors was a long time coming.

In early 1991, while NeXT and Pixar were struggling, Jobs had a new crisis in his personal life. His girlfriend Laurene Powell was pregnant.

Jobs was now thirty-six years old and far removed from the young, brash, arrogant kid he had been when Lisa was born in 1978 to his old high school girlfriend. He was serious about Powell, a second-year student in Stanford's business administration masters program, and had proposed to her at least twice, most recently during a year-end trip to Hawaii. He had given her a diamond engagement ring. But now he was waffling again.

He polled friends. He wrestled with the possibilities. He balked at the idea of marriage and then ignored the issue altogether. Frustrated, the twenty-seven-year-old Powell moved out of his house and back to her apartment for the second time in a year.

Finally, Jobs made an adult decision. On March 18, 1991, Jobs and Powell were married by his longtime spiritual adviser Kobun Chino at a lodge at Yosemite National Park. The cake was vegan and the roughly fifty people in attendance all went for a walk in the snow afterward.

Between Brenann and Powell, Jobs had a series of girlfriends. Shortly after Brennan moved to Oregon, Jobs began a relationship with a woman from Apple's public relations firm that lasted a few years. In the early 1980s, as a multimillionaire and technology heartthrob, he moved into a different social circle. For a couple of years, he dated the folk singer Joan Baez off and on, though she was fourteen years older. The Macintosh team was astonished when he brought her in to show off the top-secret project, and she attended an annual holiday party with him. Ultimately, though, the age difference was too great.

He also went out with Maya Lin, who designed the Vietnam Veterans Memorial, and had a blind date with the actress Diane Keaton. For a year, he also dated a University of Pennsylvania undergraduate named Jennifer Egan, seeing her every time he went to the East Coast. He lectured her about the need to avoid attachment to material objects, and she countered by asking him how he could justify making computers that people wanted. "We had exuberant debates about it," she said.

Egan, who became a Pulitzer Prize–winning novelist, let Jobs know she was too young for marriage and the relationship ended.

In 1984, *BusinessWeek* asked him about his personal interests, and Jobs replied, "I like films and romances."

What kinds of romance? "Young, super intelligent, artistic women. I think they're in New York rather than Silicon Valley," he said.

Jobs's first true, long-term relationship would take place with a woman he met when she was visiting the Apple office. Tina Redse was a graphic designer and the two had a long, turbulent relationship. By the mid-1980s, Jobs had purchased an old Spanish-style mansion with fourteen bedrooms and almost no furniture. She moved in with him, though he still slept on a mattress on the floor and was such a perfectionist that he wouldn't let her buy a couch. Frustrated by the lack of furniture, she eventually moved out.

Still, the two were passionate when they were together, enough so that NeXT employees recalled their "make-out sessions" in the company lobby. But they also fought bitterly, sometimes in public. Like Chrisann Brennan, Redse was put off by how cold and uncaring Jobs was at times and how hurtful he could be to her and others. She also pushed him to spend more time with his daughter, Lisa, who was now in grade school.

Ross Perot encouraged Jobs to marry Redse, and in 1989, he finally proposed. But she turned him down, deciding they could never make it work. They would, however, remain in touch.

Laurene Powell wandered into Jobs's life one fall evening when he was speaking at the Stanford Business School. She had gone with a friend, and when no other seats were available, she sat in a reserved one. When Jobs arrived, she found herself next to the guest of honor and teased that she had won a contest and the prize was dinner with him.

They visited for a few minutes after the speech and Jobs was supposed to head on to a NeXT meeting. But once in his car, he had a change of heart. "I was in the parking lot, with the key in the car, and I thought to myself, if this is my last night on earth, would I rather spend it at a business meeting, or with this woman?

"I ran across the parking lot, asked her if she'd have dinner with me. She said yes, we walked into town, and we've been together ever since," he said.

Originally from New Jersey, Powell had lost her father as a young girl and had learned to be resilient. Golden-haired, athletic, and a vegetarian, she graduated from the University

Opposite page: Steve Jobs with his wife, Laurene Powell.

of Pennsylvania and worked at the blue-chip Wall Street firm Goldman Sachs before deciding to go to business school. She had all the right qualities: intelligence, good looks, and an impressive résumé.

Their relationship also had its highs and lows, with Jobs asking her to marry him one day and then avoiding the subject for months after. She would be the center of his attention and then ignored; she would be confused by his darker sides, but endured them.

Powell was just one new family member that Jobs brought into his life during the post-Apple years. For several years after Lisa was born, Jobs avoided her and Chrisann. "I didn't want to be a father, so I wasn't," he told biographer Walter Isaacson during a series of interviews. Occasionally, he would stop by their house and talk with Chrisann, essentially ignoring his child.

But once he left Apple and was working at NeXT, closer to where they lived, he began to drop by more frequently, taking Lisa to dinner and even once bringing her to the office, where she performed cartwheels in the hallway. As she got older, they would take walks or go Rollerblading.

Still, Lisa wrote later, "My mother had raised me mostly alone. We didn't have many things but she is warm and we were happy. We moved a lot." Thirteen times, in fact. Though she knew her father was rich and famous, she only got to know him slowly. Once, when she was a young teen, he took her on a business trip to Tokyo.

Jobs had relaxed his eating habits at Apple, saying that "Interacting with people has got to be seriously balanced against living a little healthier." But after he left, he had returned to his strict vegetarian ways—though he continued to love sushi. On this trip, he took Lisa to a sushi bar in a hotel basement, where they shared trays of unagi sushi, cooked eel on rice. Some were topped with salt, some with a sweet sauce. "Both were warm and dissolved in my mouth," Lisa remembered. The distance between her and her often-absent father also dissolved. "It was the first time I'd felt, with him, so relaxed and content," she wrote. "A once inaccessible space had opened. He was less rigid with himself, even human under the great ceilings with the little chairs, with the meat, and me."

Not long after Jobs married, Lisa moved in with him and Powell and lived with them during her high school years. She would go to Harvard and become a writer. Like many of Jobs's relationships, this one would go hot and cold, with the two sometimes going months and even years without speaking. (Her college graduation was one of those times: She didn't invite him, and he didn't attend.)

One other piece of Jobs's family also fell into place.

In the mid-1980s, Clara Jobs was diagnosed with lung cancer. During visits with her, Jobs quizzed her about her past, learning that she had married before, to a man who had died in war. He also learned more details about his adoption.

Jobs resisted tracking down his birth mother because he didn't want to hurt Paul and Clara, whom he loved dearly and considered his only real parents. But after Clara died in November 1986 at the age of sixty-two, he told his father about his interest and his dad gave him the go-ahead.

Through some sleuthing and the help of a detective, Jobs was able to track down Joanne Schieble in Los Angeles. He learned that his father was Abdulfattah "John" Jandali, a Syrian who had become a political science professor. Joanne had returned to Wisconsin after Jobs's birth. After her father died, she and Jandali married and they had another child, a girl they named Mona.

Steve, it turned out, had a biological sister.

Jandali abandoned the family after just a few years, and Joanne remarried. Both she and Mona took the surname Simpson, though that marriage didn't last, either.

Jobs visited Joanne Simpson in Los Angeles, partly to thank her for giving him his life. She apologized repeatedly, saying she had always missed him.

Soon after, Jobs met Mona in New York. She had just finished a novel called *Anywhere But Here*, about her migration with her mother to Los Angeles from Wisconsin, and

The novelist Mona Simpson, who first met her brother Steve Jobs when they were in their twenties.

she was working at a literary magazine called the *Paris Review*. They hit it off immediately, discovering that they both liked long walks, were intense in their work, and notably strong-willed. While Jobs had never felt particularly close to his sister Patty, he and Mona became close friends, and she came to know his girlfriends and Lisa.

As an acclaimed novelist, she drew from personal experiences and in the mid-1990s, she wrote a book called *A Regular Guy* about a narcissistic workaholic who ignores his daughter until he is pushed out of his job. The first sentence: "He was a man too busy to flush toilets." Though it was a novel, it was clearly based on Jobs, and it was hard to know where the facts ended and the fiction began.

Mona, on her own, had begun to track down their dad, and found him in Sacramento, California. But Jobs wasn't interested in meeting him, and worried that his biological father might try to somehow blackmail him or get at his fortune. He told his sister he didn't want to be mentioned.

So Mona flew to Sacramento alone. Jandali had left teaching and was working in the restaurant business. As they talked, he told her that another child, a boy, had been born before her. "We'll never see that baby again," he told her.

He told Mona about other restaurants he had run, including a Mediterranean one near San Jose. To her complete surprise, he went on, "All of the successful technology people used to come there. Even Steve Jobs."

Jobs, Jandali continued, "was a sweet guy, and a big tipper."

It was all Mona could do not to reveal her secret—that Steve Jobs was his son.

Mona called Jobs right away and shared the remarkable story. Jobs was amazed—and he remembered the restaurant and the owner. "He was Syrian. Balding. We shook hands," he said later.

The scattered pieces of Jobs's history and his family were coming together. Then, in September 1991, Powell gave birth to a son. The couple took two weeks to give him a name: Reed Paul Jobs. "New product names are hard," the initial birth announcement said.

For Jobs, the newborn was life changing. "It's almost like a switch gets flipped inside you and you can feel a whole new range of feelings that you never thought you'd have," he said a few months later. "It's much more profound than I ever would have guessed from hearing about it."

The family moved to a new house in Palo Alto. They wanted to raise grounded children, and Mona Simpson remembered that they lived simply. In their early years, they often ate dinner on the grass and sometimes dinner "consisted of just one vegetable. Lots of that one vegetable," she said, such as broccoli, "with just the right, recently snipped, herb."

Jobs and Powell managed to buy beds and a few necessities, but little else. "We spoke about furniture in theory for eight years," Powell said. "We spent a lot of time asking ourselves, 'What is the purpose of a sofa?'"

Even buying a washing machine was an ordeal. When they decided they needed one in the mid-1990s, Jobs explained that they were impressed with European machines that use less water and are easier on clothes, but take twice as long per cycle.

"We spent some time in our family talking about what's the trade-off we want to make," he said. That involved both design and family values. "Did we care most about getting our wash done in an hour versus an hour and a half? Or did we care most about our clothes feeling really soft and lasting longer? Did we care about using a quarter of the water?"

Discussion and debate continued at the dinner table for two weeks before the family settled on machines made in Germany by Miele. "These guys really thought the process through," Job said. "I got more thrill out of them than I have out of any piece of high tech in years."

Buying a washing machine was hardly designing the Macintosh or making a dent in the universe, but Jobs was a changed man. The time after Jobs was pushed from Apple is often called his "wilderness" period because he seemed to be wandering far removed from the technology and people who made his first act so stellar. Now, in his middle age, Jobs no longer expected new technologies to revolutionize the world. "I'm sorry, it's true," he told an interviewer. "Having children really changes your view on these things. We're born, we live for a brief instant, and we die," he said. "Technology is not changing it much—if at all."

At the same time that his companies struggled, Jobs was building his first true family relationships as an adult, finally creating a real life outside of work. Because of his nature, these relationships would be complex and rocky. And his blended family was as complicated as any you could draw up, with a mother and father, plus biological parents; a sister and a biological sister; a wife and ultimately three children; and a former girlfriend and his oldest child.

Eventually, he would develop a meaningful and lasting bond with most of them—though not all. Jandali would learn from news stories that Jobs was his biological son, but he would never meet him in that role.

Paul Jobs, Steve's father, passed away in March 1993, at the age of seventy; years later, his son still called him "a great man." Asked once what he wanted to pass on to his children, Jobs said he just wanted to "try to be as good a father to them as my father was to me. I think about that every day of my life."

For his part, Paul Jobs was immensely proud of his difficult but successful son, attending his public presentations until the end.

During these challenging years, Jobs may have wandered professionally, but he clearly grew in the realm that stretches the heart and nourishes the soul—as a son, husband, and father.

And his working time wouldn't be a total loss, either.

Woodside

In the early 1990s, Jobs and Powell settled into their Palo Alto home, fitting in so easily that they often left the back door unlocked. But in the old Woodside neighborhood, Jobs ended up in a long and bitter battle over the mansion he left behind.

Jobs kept the Woodside house, a sprawling 17,000-square-foot Spanish Colonial Revival with fourteen bedrooms and thirteen-and-a-half baths, with the hope of some day tearing it down and building a smaller, simpler home there.

For some years, his family used the house and its swimming pool for parties. When President Bill Clinton and his wife, Hillary, came to visit their daughter, Chelsea, at Stanford, they stayed in another house on the wooded property.

In mid-2004, Jobs asked the town's planning commission to allow him to bulldoze the mansion, built in 1926 for copper magnate Daniel C. Jackling. Jobs said it was poorly built and called it "one of the biggest abominations of a house I've ever seen."

Neighbors, however, called it historic and argued it should be preserved.

The commission agreed to let Jobs demolish the house, but only if he tried for a year to find someone to move the structure somewhere else. The town council upheld that decision in early 2005. But the neighbors sued and a judge blocked the demolition.

Starting in about 2000, Jobs left the house open to the elements and by late in the decade, it was rotting and falling apart.

In 2009, Jobs finally got another demolition permit. To the disappointment of neighbors, the house was torn down in February 2011. By then, however, Jobs wasn't interested in building a new home.

14

Siliwood

Two years into the work on *Toy Story*, the team at Pixar had a huge problem: Woody, the main character, was a jerk. The floppy cowboy with the pull-string voice was mean, selfish, and sarcastic.

In one scene, the top toy in Andy's bedroom intentionally shoved the innocent newcomer Buzz Lightyear out the bedroom window into the evil neighbor's yard. Then Woody closed the blinds and said, "Hey, it's a toy-eat-toy world."

The Disney folks had been pushing for a character that was edgier. But they hated this guy.

After seeing a rough version of the movie in late November 1993, the president of Walt Disney animation ordered John Lasseter and his team to shut down production immediately. The film couldn't proceed unless Disney approved a

Opposite page: John Lasseter, head animator at Pixar, playing with Buzz Lightyear and Woody dolls from their first major motion picture, *Toy Story*.

new script. The first real collaboration between the glamour of Hollywood and technology of Silicon Valley—dubbed Siliwood—was on hold. All of the animation work would have to stop while the writers tried to fix the story.

The decision was frightening for the Pixar staff that had so wanted to make the first full-length computer-animated movie. And it was another setback for Steve Jobs, who had to stand behind the company and keep paying employees during the shutdown.

Already, it had been a difficult year for NeXT.

In late 1992, as buyers continued to shun NeXT's computers, several of the top people jumped ship. Jobs felt deserted and wanted to quit, too. But he just couldn't bear to endure another public failure. "Everyone here can leave—except me," he told the remaining executives.

Finally, in early 1993, Jobs listened to what his customers and managers had been telling him to do: NeXT got out of the computer business, admitting defeat in that arena. Said *Fortune:* "Jobs's dream of building another great computer manufacturer like Apple, which he cofounded, is dead, dead, dead."

NeXT let more than three hundred staffers go, keeping just two hundred, and it turned over its fabulous factory to Canon. The company would live, but as an almost insignificant seller of what some called "obscure" software.

Jobs's once-bright star diminished further.

After "a steep fall from a very lofty perch," the *Wall Street Journal* wrote in mid-1993, Jobs "is fighting to show he still matters in the computer industry."

"People have stopped paying attention to him," said Richard Shaffer, editor of *Computer Letter* told the paper. "It's sad."

Magazines called him a "flameout." Then, almost to add insult to injury, *Fortune* magazine named the onetime boy wonder as one of America's toughest bosses, leading the article with Jobs "screaming wildly" for several minutes in an "expletive-laden tirade" aimed at a manager who had told him that the black NeXT case was going to cost more than Jobs wanted to pay.

The story went on to say that the thirty-eight-year-old could be charming and a great motivator one minute and then deliver blistering attacks if something fell short of his expectations. When Jobs introduced the NeXT computer, he insisted a worker try thirty-seven different shades of green before finding the perfect one for the presentation slides.

"The highs were unbelievable," one former employee said. "But the lows were unimaginable."

Stuck in his own low, Jobs tried to find a way out. The Pixar scriptwriters were able to fix Woody's character flaws with a rewrite, but for part of 1994, Jobs tried to sell all or part of Pixar. He tried Hallmark, the card maker; Paul Allen,

Microsoft cofounder; and even Microsoft itself, but couldn't make a deal.

Then, as the movie came together and Disney agreed to distribute it during the 1995 holiday season, he had a change of heart. Thanks to the sophisticated software Pixar had developed and its clever and committed people, the movie was turning into a lovable buddy story for the ages.

It was also a marvel of technology. Using geometry, algebra, and the latest powerful computers, the animators created toys capable of fluid movement, realistic expressions, and minute details. Woody, who was based on a pull-string Casper the Friendly Ghost talking doll that Lasseter loved as a child, had more than seven hundred mathematical points that could be controlled, including more than two hundred in his face. Adding in fibers, wrinkles, dirt, bumps, and other details took thousands of hours of additional work. And animators would work for a week to make Woody's expressions match a few seconds of dialogue from actor Tom Hanks.

While changes in old-fashioned animation required actually redrawing characters, the software allowed adjustments to be made with clicks instead. Lasseter could easily refine images, instructing animators to tilt Mr. Potato Head's face "so it's easier for the baby to bite off his nose," or suggesting, "let's see if we can make the baby's slobber more elastic, so it sticks and stretches longer."

Altogether, each frame—which appeared for 1/24 of a second—would require five megabytes of memory, almost forty times more than what was in the very first Macintosh. And then pulling all the characters, backgrounds, and other details into final images would take hundreds of hours of processing on a farm of fast computers.

As the project came together, marketers signed on. Burger King agreed to promote the characters with its kids' meals and Frito-Lay placed seven-foot cutouts of Woody and Buzz in grocery stores.

In early 1995, Jobs celebrated turning forty at a bash thrown by his friend Larry Ellison, chief executive of tech company Oracle. Now, he was often driving a Jeep Cherokee instead of his Porsche, and about to be the father of another daughter, Erin Siena. But he was also excited about Pixar's creation. In May 1995, he made Fernanda and Greta Schlender, then nine and ten years old, two of the luckiest kids in America. He invited the girls and their dad, *Fortune* reporter Brent Schlender, to his house for an informal screening of *Toy Story*.

The movie wasn't nearly complete—some of it was still in black and white and without full motion—but Jobs could hardly wait to quiz the Schlender kids when it ended. "So, whatddya think? Is it as good as *Pocahontas*?"

Both girls thought it was.

"Well, then," Jobs went on, "is it as good as *The Lion King*?"

They had to think about this one. Fernanda gave the answer he wanted to hear. "To tell you the truth, I won't really be able to make up my mind until I see *Toy Story* five or six more times."

As the opening date neared, Jobs came up with a plan that was as outrageous as any he had proposed before: He would arrange to sell Pixar shares to the public shortly after the movie opened.

Even for hotshot Wall Street types who are always looking for a hot stock, the idea took an incredible amount of chutzpah. Before 1995, Pixar had modest annual revenue of up to $7.3 million from selling some expensive computers, making commercials, and selling specialized software.

True, Jobs had a deal with Disney to make two more pictures after *Toy Story*. But the company also had accumulated losses year after year.

Despite all that, Jobs expected stock buyers to spend their hard-earned money on acquiring a small piece of a company that had made one full-length movie, which might or might not be successful and which might or might not be followed by other successful movies. Industry professionals told him he was nuts.

Maybe. But he was also Steve Jobs, who didn't take no for an answer.

He hired a chief financial officer to sell the idea to Wall Street and investors. As at Apple, the notion that some people might get rich while others wouldn't caused hard feelings. Only a handful of executives—cofounder Ed Catmull, director John Lasseter, the new financial executive, and a couple of others—would own enough stock to become millionaires if the offering was successful. The rest of the staff would be able to buy stock in the future at a discount, but they wouldn't be able to actually buy their shares for up to four years. In the meantime, Steve Jobs would own about 80 percent of the company after the offering.

He had excellent timing. That summer, a small, one-year-old company called Netscape, which had developed one of the first browsers for searching the Web, was able to successfully sell stock to the public, despite its short history. Suddenly, an offering of Pixar shares looked promising.

Toy Story opened on Thanksgiving weekend of 1995 to enthusiastic reviews, and families rushed to see it. It brought in $29 million its first weekend, breaking the record for Thanksgiving debuts. And it became the box office hit of the year, selling $192 million in tickets in the United States and almost as much overseas.

A week later, Pixar stock was sold to the public at $22 a share. On the first day of trading, the stock more than doubled in price before closing at $39 a share. The offering brought in more than $130 million for the company to fund its future business.

Even more remarkable, Steve Jobs, the onetime personal-computer whiz kid who had staked a significant part of his fortune on keeping the company afloat, briefly owned stock worth more than $1 billion, before the price fell back to earth.

The scriptwriters at Pixar couldn't have come up with a better ending.

Yet even as Jobs relished the success of *Toy Story* and enjoyed his growing family, Apple never was far from his heart or mind. "Anybody who knows him well," wrote *Fortune* reporter Schlender, "will tell you that rarely a day goes by when he doesn't think about what he would do if he were running Apple."

Apple had grown solidly for several years under Sculley, but it stumbled in the early 1990s and Sculley was pushed out in 1993. Under his successor, the company's troubles grew.

While it took about a decade, Microsoft finally figured out how to copy the best features of the Macintosh and even improve on some. In the meantime, Apple technology had gone stale. In an interview, Jobs was critical: "The desktop computer industry is dead. Innovation has virtually ceased. Microsoft dominates with very little innovation.

"Apple lost," he said.

In fall 1995, he confided to *Fortune,* "You know, I've got a plan that could rescue Apple." He wouldn't give details, but said, "It's the perfect product and the perfect strategy for Apple. But nobody there will listen to me. . . ."

Now, with his enormous success at Pixar, maybe someone would listen after all.

Jungle Cruise

John Lasseter, the genius behind the *Toy Story* and *Cars* movies, credits a summer job at Disneyland with helping prepare him.

Lasseter loved cartoons from the time he was a little kid. Every Saturday, he was up at 6:30 a.m. to catch the first shows after the farm report. In high school, he raced home from water polo practice to see Bugs Bunny. His mother, an art teacher, encouraged him.

As a freshman in high school, he ran across a book called *The Art of Animation* and realized for the first time that he might be able to make a living in animation. He studied art and was invited to study animation at a new program at the California Institute of the Arts.

But he says a lot of what he knows about comedy and comedic timing came from a summer job as a Jungle Cruise ride operator at Disneyland. "I learned that the worse the puns and the jokes, the funnier they could be, if you knew how to deliver them," he said. One of his favorites involved a group of "natives" on a pole, who were escaping a rhino in the water.

"You'd come up and say, 'Oh, there they are, it's the famous Hontas tribe. They've been lost for a long time,'" he said.

And then, the punch line: "'Oh, look, the rhino is trying to . . . poca-a-Hontas!'"

What's Geometry Got to Do with It?

Computer animation takes not only an understanding of computers, but also a heaping dose of math and physics to create a believable virtual world.

"This whole world only exists because of mathematics. Everything you do in it is a mathematical operation," said Rob Cook, a retired Pixar vice president, who wrote some of the key software. "If we do our jobs right, nobody knows that."

Consider an elbow. When it bends, the arm, hand, and wrist rotate and the bicep flexes—all mathematical equations. In both animation and video-game graphics, trigonometry helps with rotation and motion, algebra is used in special effects, and integral calculus is necessary so that lighting looks real.

To make complex three-dimensional images, points are chosen to define various shapes, essentially breaking them into polygons. Because those shapes are bumpy and inflexible, the polygons are divided and curved, until the image looks smooth and realistic. The technique, called "subdivision surface," was pioneered at Pixar.

With each film, Pixar's team was challenged to develop something new in computer animation: *A Bug's Life* needed realistic trees and leaves; *Monsters, Inc.* had lots of clothing and hair; *Finding Nemo* required splashing water, and *The Incredibles* had a cast of humans with powerful muscles.

In addition to engineers and creative storytellers, Pixar employs several PhDs, such as a physicist who specializes in air and water. The company uses "cartoon physics," Cook said, which isn't technically precise like the real thing, but allows the films to look realistic while also capturing the exaggerated double takes and bendable characters that make cartoons fun to watch.

The entrance to Apple's campus in Cupertino, California. [Photo by Joe Ravi/Creative Commons Attribution-Share Alike]

15

Return

The story that Steve Jobs told to the Stanford graduates about love and loss had a bit more to it.

Leaving Apple hurt Jobs deeply. But, he said, "Getting fired from Apple was the best thing that could have ever happened to me."

From that low point, he could make a fresh start. He founded NeXT, funded Pixar, and met "an amazing woman," his wife, Laurene.

And then, something even more remarkable happened.

In 1996, Apple needed help. It had too many of some products and not enough of others—and worse, some of its new laptops occasionally burst into flames because of faulty batteries. Apple had spent hundreds of millions of dollars working on a new operating system, code-named Copland, to replace a musty, dated one. But the development was way behind and the product was plagued with problems. Though Apple had peaked at $11 billion in annual sales for fiscal 1995, customers were disappearing and it was in such poor shape that its leaders were trying to sell it to almost anyone—even its boring and unimaginative competitor IBM.

Time called it "a chaotic mess without a strategic vision and certainly no future." *BusinessWeek* titled a cover story: "The Fall of an American Icon." Said *Fortune,* "It's enough to break your heart."

None of the talks turned into a deal. A new chief executive, Gil Amelio, was named and it appeared he needed something close to a miracle to turn the company around. Apple still had an immensely loyal following of more than twenty million people who had bought Macintosh computers, but they would soon begin switching to cheaper computers with Intel chips and Microsoft's Windows operating systems if Apple didn't offer them something better.

In the summer and into the fall, Apple's leaders looked for a magic bullet, someone or some company that could bring the kind of sophisticated software it needed to renovate and invigorate its operating system and propel its machines back to technology's front lines. For a time, it considered a small, untested company started by a former Apple executive. Then Apple got a phone call from some mid-level NeXT managers who, acting on their own, suggested they look at NeXT. The pairing made sense; given that NeXT was built by Jobs and other former Apple managers, the two companies practically shared genetic material.

Jobs had been spending more time at Pixar and he was open to selling Apple the NeXT software or the whole company, which was still losing money.

In December 1996, Jobs returned to Apple's Cupertino campus for the first time since he left in 1985, bringing his substantial charm and spellbinding sales skills along. Over a couple of sessions, he wowed Apple's leaders with NeXT's dazzling abilities and covered company whiteboards with his vision of how the software could make Apple's computers more nimble for Internet programmers and users. Amelio and his team were sold.

In late December, in another Pixar-like ending, Apple agreed to buy NeXT for more than $400 million. It was a surprisingly rich price; though it was ten years old, NeXT was unprofitable and had only about $47 million in sales—what Apple brought in during its third year of existence. But Apple was buying more than software; it was also getting Steve Jobs, its visionary founder, who agreed to serve as an adviser to Amelio.

Financially, Jobs did well, too, of course: For his ownership of NeXT, he would receive $130 million in cash and 1.5

million shares of Apple stock, worth about $22.5 million. (The rest of the money would go to other NeXT shareholders.)

In early January, both Amelio and Jobs appeared at the big Macworld convention in San Francisco, a conference that at the time brought together Macintosh's biggest fans twice a year to share ideas and see innovations. More than four thousand people—computer users, educators, professionals, software developers, and others—jammed into a ballroom to see the keynote presentation. With computer sales sliding sharply, they were looking for some good news.

Amelio, who skipped the chance to practice his speech, rambled, droning on well beyond his allotted time. Finally, he introduced Jobs.

As he came onstage, Macintosh fans leaped to their feet and screamed. Cameras flashed, and they welcomed their wandering founder with a long ovation. "The return of Elvis would not have provoked a bigger sensation," wrote reporter Jim Carlton. In a short, succinct presentation, Jobs demonstrated how NeXT would bring new energy to the dated machines.

After the conference, Jobs and Amelio were in regular touch, and by February, two of Jobs's lieutenants were moved into top Apple positions. By then, Jobs had decided Amelio was, like Sculley before him, a bozo.

Though the NeXT software would eventually help Apple rejuvenate its computers, doing so would take a few years. In the meantime, Apple's problems continued to grow. It customers were abandoning its computers, and red ink was flowing, so much so that its losses would reach well over $1.5 billion. Many people believed it was close to catastrophe.

Jobs began to lose patience. In June 1997, he sold the 1.5 million shares he had gotten for NeXT for about $15 a share, leaving him, again, with just one share of Apple. "I pretty much had given up hope that the Apple board was going to do anything," he said.

He should have waited. Perhaps spurred on by Jobs's blunt assessment of the boss, Apple's board decided it had seen enough. Gil Amelio was removed as chief executive officer in early July 1997. Jobs's advisory role was expanded.

That day, the top executives of Apple were summoned to a conference room. Amelio stood in front of the group and told them, "It's time for me to move on." He wished them well and left.

A few minutes later, Jobs walked in and sat down. He was wearing shorts, sneakers, and a few days of stubble. "Okay, tell me what's wrong with this place," he asked the group. A few offered responses.

Jobs cut to the point: "It's the products!" he declared. "So what's wrong with the products?"

More mumbled answers. He stopped them with his own definitive answer:

"The products SUCK!"

Almost exactly twelve years before, the boy wonder had been pushed out of the company he cofounded, built, promoted, and loved. Now, at forty-two years old, he was back.

Before too long, he would become Apple's interim chief executive, a job he would call "iCEO," a nod to the products Apple would soon be rolling out.

He never ran Apple the first time, and he had never run a company anywhere near as large as Apple had become, especially not one that was rapidly moving toward an epic failure. But this was no longer the brash, impulsive, bratty kid who had been pushed out. The family man with three children had learned a few things.

He was still intense and passionate, and he could still be painfully blunt and harsh. He could still be mean, even to those he loved most. But he was also learning to sometimes see things from another point of view. As he moved to prune the bloated Apple enterprise, for instance, he found that laying off or firing people was "harder for me now. Much harder."

He did it because he believed his job required him to. But, he said, he realized "that person could be me coming home to tell my wife and kids that I just got laid off. Or that could be one of my kids in twenty years. I never took it so personally before."

At NeXT he had been humbled by his failure to capture lightning in a bottle a second time. At Pixar, where he was more the banker than the boss, he learned to let the artists be the artists—and something more.

Initially, said Pamela Kerwin, a Pixar vice president, Jobs would dominate meetings, cutting people off to say, "Okay, here's how I see things." But now, she said, "He listens a lot more, and he's more relaxed, more mature."

Jobs saw it another way. "I trust people more," he said.

In an almost unbelievable way, the dots had connected again. Jobs had been thrown out of Apple, started a company that struggled, and then sold that company to Apple, his first love, where he was now in charge. Of course, none of it would have happened had he not been fired.

In his speech to the Stanford graduates, he warned that they would have painful setbacks as well. "Sometimes life hits you in the head with a brick. Don't lose faith," he told them. His most important choice was remaining true to what he loved, he said, whether it was work or a life partner.

If they hadn't found that love yet, he told them, "Keep looking until you find it. Don't settle."

In the coming years, Jobs would face challenges and

crises he couldn't begin to imagine. But he never settled for doing something he didn't love.

He did, however, start his new Apple job with a most unusual deal—settling a very old rivalry.

Steve's Uniform

Starting in the late 1990s and for the rest of his life, Jobs was often seen dressed in the same clothing: a black mock turtleneck, Levis, and well-worn New Balance shoes.

Jobs said he initially was inspired by a 1980s trip to Sony, the large Japanese consumer electronics company, where everyone wore uniforms. The company explained that after World War II, many workers didn't have clothes. So employers came up with uniforms so employees would have things to wear. Over time, those uniforms bonded workers with their company.

Jobs thought such a uniform would be great for Apple—but his American team quickly shot him down.

Still, Jobs became friends with fashion designer Issey Miyake, who had designed some Sony uniforms, and asked him to make some black turtlenecks that he liked. "He made me, like, a hundred of them," Jobs said, showing biographer Walter Isaacson a stack in his closet.

The turtleneck and jeans (no belt, please) became Jobs's primary personal uniform—though he sometimes wore cargo shorts and sandals or padded around barefoot. The routine made getting dressed each day exceptionally easy while conveying Jobs's personal image to the world.

The image of Bill Gates overwhelms the stage as Steve Jobs announces an agreement for Microsoft to invest in Apple.

16

Different

Long before there was a well-known word for it, Steve Jobs and Bill Gates were frenemies. But now Apple was at a critical crossroads, and Jobs needed to put his differences aside.

The two had a long and complex history. Both were born in 1955, and won fame in their early twenties—Jobs in personal computers and Gates in software. Early on, Microsoft wrote a key program for the Apple II and initially created the spreadsheet program Excel for the Macintosh, launching its own business making add-on software. As bachelors into their later thirties, they even went on some double dates.

Gates saw personal computers as something that would make businesses run better. Jobs saw them as a "remarkable tool" that could make humans better. Gates, who is practical and methodical, was willing to move an okay product out the door and improve on it later. Jobs, the emotional and mercurial one, didn't want to ship until his work was perfect.

Jobs, dashing and charismatic, was the first to become a millionaire and became the face of the technology revolution. But once Microsoft sold stock to the public, Gates's shares soared so high and so fast that he was soon among the very wealthiest people in America. At times, they each wanted what the other had: Gates, the true computer nerd, resented that Jobs didn't even know how to write software code but was considered a brilliant technology visionary. And Jobs, who was a tough negotiator and hard-driving executive, resented that Gates was considered a savvier businessman.

They also had a long and bitter fight over whether Gates and Microsoft stole the most clever parts of the Macintosh for the Windows operating system. Apple fought Microsoft over the issue in the courts for years, but lost.

At times, each was downright catty about the other. While Gates was a vocal supporter of Macintosh, he sneered at the work Jobs did at NeXT. When he was asked if Microsoft would develop software for the new computer, he responded, "Develop for it? I'll piss on it."

Jobs was just as snarky about Gates's success. In a 1994 *Rolling Stone* interview, after Gates was named the richest man in America, Jobs was asked how he felt about Gates becoming so successful with software that had mimicked Apple's. Jobs responded, "You know, the goal is not to be the richest man in the cemetery. It's not my goal anyway."

A few years later, in a television interview, he was brutally blunt in describing Microsoft. "They just have no taste," he said. "I don't mean that in a small way. I mean that in a big way, in the sense that they don't think of original ideas and they don't bring much culture into their products." Jobs conceded that Microsoft had mostly earned its success. But, he added, "I have a problem with the fact that they just make really third-rate products."

After the interview, he apologized to Gates, saying he should never have shared his opinion in public. But then, Jobs went on to tell a reporter that he thought Gates was "a bit narrow" and would be a broader person if he had "gone off to an ashram when he was younger."

By the late 1990s, Apple's faithful Mac owners had come to see their company as the Luke Skywalker to Microsoft's Darth Vader in the ongoing battle for computer craftsmanship and friendliness. But with Macintosh sales dropping like a rock and its new operating system up in the air, Microsoft wouldn't commit to continuing to make its popular Excel and Word programs for Mac, which required different software than Windows. (That's still true, though it matters a lot less now that so much content comes over the Internet.)

The Apple software was a good business for Microsoft, but not crucial for it. Without Microsoft's products, however, Apple would, quite literally, rot.

One of Jobs's first moves after Amelio left was to call Gates. "I'm going to turn this thing around," he told him. But, he said frankly, "I need help."

In negotiations that included a long walk with a Microsoft financial executive and a barefoot Jobs, the two sides quickly reached a deal. Microsoft would continue to make its software for the Mac and would pay an undisclosed amount of money to settle simmering patent disputes. On top of that, Microsoft would buy $150 million of Apple's stock.

To maximize the drama, Jobs planned to make the announcement at a summer Macworld convention in Boston. During rehearsals, Jobs tied up the final details of the deal with Gates on a cell phone. A photographer overheard his grateful words, which would appear on the cover of *Time* magazine: "Bill, thank you for your support of this company," he said. "I think the world's a better place for it."

The devoted Macworld crowd was thrilled to see Jobs again—until he began to spell out the Microsoft deal. They were unconvinced when he told them the time for "competition between Apple and Microsoft is over." When he said that Microsoft's Internet Explorer would be the Internet browser sold as part of the Mac, they groaned. And when Bill Gates's smug mug appeared on the giant screen in the auditorium, the audience broke into boos and hisses.

Later, Jobs admitted that he had botched the staging, that

he and Apple looked small next to the giant image of Gates's face. Gates, too, was embarrassed when he saw a video of his enormous face on the screen. But the point was made: Microsoft was making a tiny investment for a company its size, but it was telling the world that it believed Apple would be around in the future. Wall Street got the message. Apple's stock shot up that day as investors concluded it would, indeed, be a survivor.

Though Jobs wouldn't officially be the interim CEO for a few weeks, he wasted no time making other radical moves. His chutzpah still intact, he asked most of the board of directors to resign, including Mike Markkula, the original investor, who had been with the company from the beginning. The old members were replaced with directors who saw the world Jobs's way, including his good friend Larry Ellison, the head of software maker Oracle, and Bill Campbell, a former Apple marketing executive now running another software company.

Internally, Jobs continued Amelio's efforts to cut costs dramatically in order to keep the company afloat. He ditched Apple's printer business and killed a handheld device called Newton. He studied Apple's bloated line of a dozen computers and then drew a two-by-two grid on a white board. Apple would make four main products and that would be it— desktop and laptop computers for businesses and desktop and laptop computers for consumers.

He imposed new rules at headquarters, such as banning dogs at work. Jobs, a vegan who ate granola in apple juice for breakfast, even replaced the cafeteria staff, calling their work "dog food." Tofu began to appear on the menu.

While Apple wouldn't have new products or a truly new operating system for a while, Jobs instinctively knew he needed to change the way the world—and even his own employees—saw his baby. Just as he had gone back to his old pal Bill Gates, he turned to the advertising folks who had made the Macintosh "1984" ad to work their magic again.

Jobs didn't want to promote products. Rather, he wanted to portray the company's values, in the same way Nike celebrated athletics and athletes without ever mentioning its shoes. "Our customers want to know, 'Who is Apple?' and 'What is it we stand for?' Where do we fit in this world?" he explained—dressed in his typical black mock turtleneck, shorts, and sandals—to one gathering. "What we're about isn't about making boxes for people to get their jobs done, although we do that well," he said. "Apple is about something more than that."

The ad team, now called TBWA\Chiat\Day, concluded that Apple didn't follow the rules that others did. It wasn't like other companies. Fairly quickly, it came up with a tagline: "Think Different."

But how could advertisements portray that? The team tried Apple customers, film clips, even mice. In a burst of inspiration it decided to celebrate creativity, the remarkable people—living and dead—who had the passion to change the world for the better. As Jobs would say about the ones no longer living: "If they ever used a computer, it would have been a Mac."

Jobs was critical of the first draft, of course, but even contributed a line to the final free-verse poem of the television ad. It went like this:

> *Here's to the crazy ones. The misfits. The rebels. The troublemakers.*
>
> *The round pegs in the square holes. The ones who see things differently.*
>
> *They're not fond of rules. And they have no respect for the status quo. You can quote them, disagree with them, glorify or vilify them.*
>
> *About the only thing you can't do is ignore them. Because they change things. They push the human race forward.*
>
> *While some may see them as the crazy ones, we see genius. Because the people who are crazy enough to think they can change the world are the ones who do.*

Accompanying the narrative were images of geniuses of all kinds: scientist Albert Einstein, artist Pablo Picasso, Reverend Martin Luther King, Jr., dancer Martha Graham, inventor Thomas Edison, singer Bob Dylan, John Lennon and Yoko Ono, aviator Amelia Earhart, puppeteer Jim Henson, and many others. The ad ended with a black screen and the tagline "Think Different," with the colorful Apple logo.

The television ad would win an Emmy, and the print and television campaign would run effectively for five years. It deeply moved Jobs. When he first showed it to a *Newsweek* reporter, he cried. He choked up again as he described it to biographer Walter Isaacson. "Every once in a while, I find myself in the presence of purity—purity of spirit and love—and I always cry. It always just reaches in and grabs me," he said. "There was a purity about that I will never forget."

There was also a not-so-small problem: The slogan would cause English teachers to break out in hives. The phrase "Think Different" wasn't grammatically correct. The proper use should have been "Think Differently." This was particularly an issue for Apple, which sold more computers to schools and college students than any other company.

Jobs and the team wrestled with the language. Ultimately, Jobs wanted "different" to be seen as a noun, as in "think big," or "think victory." Using "differently," an adverb, would send "an unintended message. It would tell the reader HOW to think," according to a note the ad team prepared to answer those who complained. Instead, Apple wanted the slogan to tell us "what to think about."

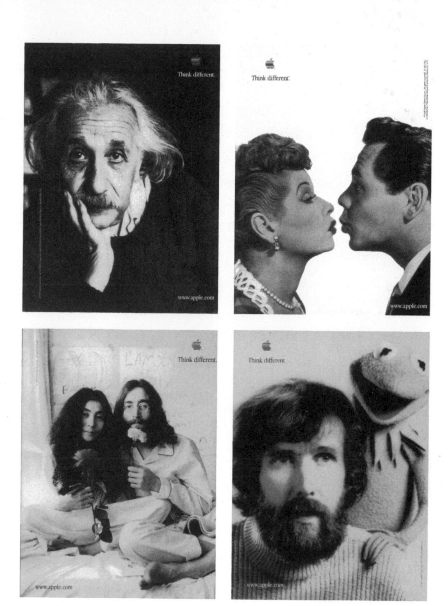

Apple's "Think Different" campaign (which ran both in print and on television) didn't try to sell a specific product. Instead it celebrated creativity by linking the Apple brand name to extraordinary people.

After receiving the explanation, one English teacher wrote back to say she gave the company an "A+" for being "well-prepared."

The work paid off for the ad team. But for Jobs to really fix Apple, he needed to show the world products that proved Apple could, indeed, "think different."

Steve and Bill Onstage

In 2007, Steve Jobs and Bill Gates agreed to a rare joint interview at the *Wall Street Journal*'s All Things Digital Conference, bringing together Mac and PC publicly. Toward the end of their session, someone asked what each learned from the other.

Though Jobs famously criticized Gates's taste, Gates was good natured in citing his rival's "intuitive taste, both for people and products." Gates said he approached products from an engineering point of view, but Jobs would "make the decision based on a sense of people and products that, you know, is even hard for me to explain. The way he does things is just different, and I think it's magical."

Jobs, for his part, said he was impressed with how Microsoft collaborated with others. "Because Woz and I started the company based on doing the whole banana, we weren't so good at partnering with people," he said. "Bill and Microsoft were really good at it because they didn't make the whole thing in the early days, and they learned how to partner with people really well."

A little more of that trait might have served Apple well, he said.

The two were also asked about the greatest misunderstanding in their long relationship.

Gates noted that he had a lot of fun working with Jobs on projects like the Mac. Jobs noted that when they started out, they were both the youngest people in the room. Now, he said, they're often the oldest guys in the room.

"And, you know," he went on, "I think of most things in life as either a Bob Dylan or a Beatles song, but there's that one line in that one Beatles song, 'you and I have memories longer than the road that stretches out ahead.' And that's clearly true here."

17

Turnaround

For Jobs, the last part of 1997 was grueling. He finished work late at night, arriving home at about ten p.m. and falling into bed. Then, he'd get up at six a.m., shower, and do it all over again.

"I'd never been so tired in my life," he said. He was overhauling Apple and keeping an eye on Pixar, and the combination left him so exhausted that he couldn't even talk with Powell when he got home. Luckily, she understood. "She supported me and kept the family together with a husband in absentia," he said.

More remarkable, Jobs was running Apple without a paycheck. He agreed to a salary of just $1 a year, enough that his family could take advantage of the health plan. He owned just one share of stock, and he didn't receive any other stock or compensation. He told people he didn't want anything

Opposite page: Steve Jobs posing with the iMac, known for its colorful case and unique triangular shape.

more. "Bottom line is, I didn't return to Apple to make a fortune," he said (though, of course, he already was worth a fortune thanks to Pixar.) "I just wanted to see if we could work together to turn this thing around."

Many in the industry were skeptical that Apple could be fixed. When Jobs took over, it was running short on cash and it appeared to be heading toward bankruptcy. Nearly everyone was buying computers with Intel chips and Windows software, and Hewlett-Packard and Dell Computer were growing by leaps and bounds selling nondescript, low-cost machines. The market would be so price driven that eventually even IBM would sell its PC business.

At a conference, Dell founder Michael S. Dell was asked what he would do if he were in Jobs's shoes. He was blunt, saying, "I'd shut it down and give the money back to shareholders."

But Jobs, true to his original vision for Apple, believed there was room for beauty and art amid technology and commerce. He was also happy to let Dell, H-P, and others have the big and boring market for cubicle dwellers and tech dweebs while he catered to individuals. "The roots of Apple were to build computers for people, not for corporations," he said.

While no one had successfully carved out a market just for "people," he didn't see why Apple couldn't. After all, he said, the Gap was plenty successful as a retailer, and it didn't sell suits.

To begin work on a new Macintosh, he turned to Apple's top designer, Jonathan Ive, known as Jony (and pronounced "Johnny"). Jobs ordered up a computer that sounded a lot like his 1984 Macintosh: It had to be easy to use, include a keyboard and screen, work right out of the box, and cost less than $2,000, making it the cheapest machine in Apple's line.

After a couple of rejections by the boss, Ive's team came up with a box shaped more like a triangular pillow than a cube. Encasing the computer and the keyboard in a translucent plastic that exposed their innards to the world, the whole package seemed playful and inviting. The team visited a jelly bean factory to learn more about translucent colors and settled on a greenish-blue hue for the computer itself, though other candy-colored shades would be added later.

Jobs was thrilled with his out-of-the-box creation, which he saw as the essence of great design. Most people, he said, see design as the way something looks, such as "the fabric of the curtains and the sofa," he explained. But to him, "design is the fundamental soul of a man-made creation that ends up expressing itself in successive outer layers of the product or service." It's not just what a product looks like or how it feels, but how it actually works, he said. So the new machine wasn't about "just the color or translucence or the shape of the shell. The essence

iCandy.

Think different.

The iMac's bright translucent colors were inspired by a visit to a jelly bean factory. The "iCandy" ad campaign alluded to this and emphasized to consumers that this computer was different—cuter, friendlier, and more fun.

of the iMac is to be the finest possible consumer computer in which each element plays together."

Apple's engineers, however, weren't impressed with such philosophical thinking. "They came up with thirty-eight reasons" why the design didn't work, Jobs recalled. But he was the iCEO and he insisted that it could—and would—be done. So it was.

The "i" in the new iMac was presumably for Internet, but also for "individual, instruct, inform, inspire."

While Jobs's latest computer was perfect in his eyes, it had some quirks. It came with a mouse shaped like a hockey puck, which would eventually be changed to something more traditional. Jobs left out a floppy disk drive, which was commonly used for backing up and sharing files. (As a result, customers would have to buy a separate floppy drive.) He threw a five-star hissy fit when he discovered that the computer's compact-disc player was a tray that popped out rather than an elegant slot, like those found in cars today. After almost threatening to delay the computer, he forced the manufacturing executive in charge to promise that future versions wouldn't have a tray.

While the new machine was coming to life, Jobs had some good news to report to Apple lovers. In January, at the winter Macworld gathering, he told the crowd that some operating system improvements were coming, as well as new Mac software from Microsoft. Then, in what would become a classic Jobs move, he saved the best for last.

"Oh, and one more thing," he said. After months of losses, Apple would be reporting a profit for the quarter that had ended in December, the first glimmers of hope for a true turnaround. All that cost cutting had helped put the company on firmer ground.

The next glimmers would come in May 1998, when Jobs formally unveiled the new, colorful $1,299 iMacs before a crowd that included Wozniak, Markkula, and many of the original Mac team. In a throwback to his first Macintosh launch, he wore a suit instead of a turtleneck, and pulled off a cloth to reveal the adorable computer with a screen that read, "Hello (again)."

"It looks like it's from another planet—a good planet," he said. "One with better designers."

Reviewers described the machine as balloony, cartoony,

and huggable. And consumers adored it. In the first six weeks after it went on sale in August, Apple sold close to three hundred thousand iMacs, the fastest start ever for a new model. Apple's stock price rose again, reaching a level that was triple the price when Amelio departed.

Even better, a survey found that almost three out of every ten iMac buyers had never owned a computer before and more than one in ten buyers was switching to an iMac from a Windows-based machine. The timing was just right; more and more people were eager to discover the possibilities of the expanding Internet and innovations, such as e-mail, America Online's new instant messenger, and budding Web stores like Amazon and eBay.

After selling almost two *million* iMacs in the first year they were available, Apple rolled out candy-colored laptops called iBooks in mid-1999. Jobs also showed off how Apple had adopted a new technology call Wi-Fi, which allowed users to connect to the Internet without a cable.

To demonstrate the wireless Internet for *Newsweek* reporter Steven Levy, Jobs snatched up a laptop and held it like a waiter balancing a tray, illustrating how the computer could move around the room while remaining online. "Jobs was literally dancing, hips swaying in a joyous mambo around the conference table," Levy wrote.

"Isn't this why we got into this business in the first place?"

Jobs asked. "Look at what we're doing here!" Yes, Levy said, this was Silicon Valley's best showman—but also "the ultimate Apple fanboy."

A year later, Jobs took an even bigger gamble, introducing an intriguing solid black cube that looked more like a sculpture than a computer. Reminiscent of the NeXT machine, the Power Mac G4 Cube was priced more like a sculpture, too, at $3,000 with a monitor and keyboard and aimed at users who wanted more than home equipment.

Jobs had matured, but he hadn't mellowed much. He still parked in the handicapped spots and his Mercedes still lacked license plates, which apparently kept him from getting parking tickets. "It's a little game I play," he told *Fortune* magazine. In private chats, he shared his joy that his youngest daughter, Eve, born in 1998, was now waving as he left for work, but then added that he didn't let his kids watch television, which might dull their creativity.

He was still Ping-Ponging from Apple to Pixar, but less frantically. Pixar had scored another hit with *A Bug's Life* in 1998 and *Toy Story 2* would be the blockbuster of the 1999 holiday season, with the two selling more than $800 million in tickets worldwide. Though he had less to worry about than before, Jobs was up at six, answering e-mails and working before the kids got up, and then helping with breakfast and the off-to-school routine. When he could, he would work from home for another hour, landing at Apple by eight or nine. Over lunch, he might handle a few dozen Pixar calls and e-mails, and by the end of the day, he would have fielded hundreds more messages, many from Mac customers who wanted to share their thoughts with their CEO.

In the midst of all the forward motion, Jobs made a big decision. He took a walk with his wife, and explained how Apple could be a base for doing the things he wanted to do. He was ready to drop the "interim" from his title and become Apple's full-time, full-fledged chief executive. He told her that he planned to stay another four to five years.

The Apple board had been encouraging him to do so and to entice him, it offered him options to buy fourteen million shares of Apple stock. A common perk for executives and some employees, stock options usually allow the holder to buy stock in the future at today's price. So for every dollar that Apple's stock went up above the original price, Jobs would make $14 million in profit.

But despite his early insistence that he wasn't at Apple to get rich, Jobs wanted more. "What I really need is a plane where I can take my family to Hawaii on vacation," he said. He hated flying commercial airlines, especially with three young kids. The board agreed to buy him a Gulfstream V, a jet that could carry sixteen people. The gift cost Apple $88 million, including taxes it paid on Jobs's behalf, a nice present for two and half years of amazing work.

In addition to that, Jobs asked for options to buy twenty million shares of stock—even more than he had been offered. Ultimately, the board agreed to give him two grants, some shares that could be sold immediately at a profit and some that he could sell later. Though he wouldn't get the stock all at once, *Fortune* magazine valued the whole package at $381 million. Even for all he had done, it was an incredibly generous payday.

At the 2000 Macworld meeting, Jobs told the crowd that Apple would soon be introducing a new operating system based on the NeXT software it had acquired. And again, he saved the best news for last. When he told the crowd that he was dropping the "interim" from his title, the assembled jumped to their feet, chanting, "Steve, Steve, Steve!"

With a smile, Jobs accepted the ovation, but pointed out that he was part of a team. "I accept your thanks on behalf of everybody at Apple," he added.

Unfortunately, Team Apple would soon fumble. The iMac, which had been so hot, began to go stale. The fancy and elegant Apple Power Mac G4 Cube computer, introduced in summer 2000, was too expensive. It sold only half as many units as expected in the first few months, and then sales cratered. The Cube would soon be put on ice, Jobs's first big failure since his return.

By 2001, the economy was slowing, once-hot technology companies were cooling, and Apple was losing money again.

The Fifth Avenue Apple Store in New York City.

Once again, critics warned that there might not be room for a company that was so very different.

At the same time, Jobs was thinking about moving Apple into a totally new business. The big computer and electronics retailers weren't doing a very good job selling his unusual computers and they weren't likely to ever give them much attention. "I started to get scared," Jobs said. "It was like, 'We have to do something.'"

Getting into the retail business, however, was a big gamble. Jobs asked Millard "Mickey" Drexler, then the president of Gap, to join the Apple board, and he lured Ron Johnson from the Target chain to design Apple stores. At Drexler's suggestion, they built a sample store to see what looked best.

Johnson came up with the idea of a Genius Bar, which acts much like a concierge desk in a hotel, giving a hand to those who are lost, confused, or in need of help.

As with so many Apple products, Jobs was near the launch of the first Apple store when Johnson had a painful realization. The prototype store was organized by products, but customers make buying decision based on what they can do with those products, such as making videos or entertaining their kids. Redesigning the store set the launch back several months, Jobs said, "But it was the right decision by a million miles."

The first two minimalist stores, in Tyson's Corner, Virginia, and Glendale, California, opened in spring 2001.

Without hot products, however, there would be very little for Jobs to sell.

Packaging

No detail was too small for Steve Jobs to fuss over.

In addition to demanding beautiful, well-designed products, he also demanded beautiful, well-designed packages. He and Apple's top designer, Jony Ive, obsessed over just the right fold-open boxes with just-the right size slots. A computer should lift from the box in an exciting way, or a new iPod or iPhone should nestle dramatically in a plastic slip.

"Packaging can be theater, it can create a story," Ive said.

In fact, among the patents that Jobs and Ive shared were several for designs of iPod and iPhone boxes. Altogether, Jobs's name would appear on three hundred and thirteen Apple patents, covering clasps, designs, power cords, and that graceful glass staircase.

The boxes are so elegant that some fans can't part with them, storing them in closets or displaying them on shelves. There are even online photo galleries of new owners proudly undressing their latest Apple purchase.

Jobs said he began to pay attention to packaging after Mike Markkula, his mentor and Apple's first investor, told him early on that people "*DO* judge a book by its cover," and that sloppy or shoddy presentation will sully even the most wonderful products.

"When you open the box of an iPhone or iPad, we want that tactile experience to set the tone for how you perceive the product," Jobs said. "Mike taught me that."

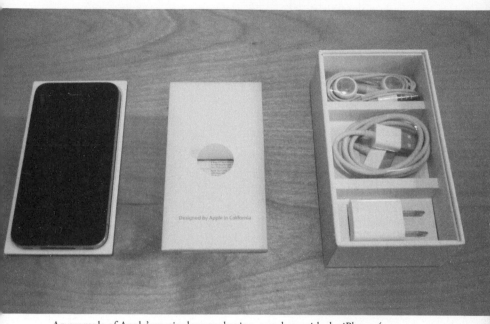

An example of Apple's meticulous packaging, seen here with the iPhone 4.

Steve Jobs standing in front of one of the iconic iPod ads as he gives a keynote address.

18

Music

In mid-2000, Jobs had yet another big problem on his hands. Apple had been developing wonderful movie-making software that would allow Mac users to easily edit their own videos and fix up their photos.

But his customers didn't want that. What they wanted was to make their own music compact discs.

Sales of the iMac had slowed down in part because the computers didn't have drives that could burn CDs. Why? Because the first CD burners had those icky trays that Jobs disliked so much, so the iMac couldn't easily be changed.

Moreover, Jobs had simply missed the revolution taking place in music. Young people—roughly the same age as Jobs and Woz when they built the first Apple—had figured out how to share digital music files, trading millions of songs without paying for them. A little upstart called Napster was turning the music business upside down.

Jobs, a man who truly loved music, had a Homer Simpson "Doh!" moment. "I felt like a dope," he said when he finally looked up and saw that millions of people were making their own CDs without any help from Apple. "I thought we had missed it. We had to work to catch up."

Quickly, teams were mobilized. Designers and engineers worked to get CD burners into all the company's computers, a job that would take until mid-2001 to complete.

Next, the computers would need some kind of "jukebox" software to help music lovers upload, search for, and sort their CDs and other music. Apple didn't have anything in house. But a small team of former Apple employees had already begun making music software. Apple acquired the business, called SoundJam, and set about imposing its own creative standards. Complex features were thrown out, buttons were simplified and made sleek, and Jobs demanded a single plain search box instead of asking users to choose an artist or an album.

Moved by what he was seeing take place, Jobs was ready to declare a new vision for Apple and the computer business at the Macworld show in early 2001. The industry was about to enter a new era, he told the group. The first wave of computing had started in 1980, with the creation of spreadsheet and word-processing software, making a desktop computer useful. That period ended in the mid-1990s, when the Internet brought a raft of new uses to both individuals and businesses.

In the new century, he said, personal computers were entering a third era, where they would be "the digital hub of our emerging digital lifestyle." Instead of simply being a tool for words and numbers, our computers would seamlessly connect us with our photos, videos, music, phones, and calendars, allowing us to keep track of, organize, and edit our digital lives.

To support that world, Apple introduced iDVD and iTunes software, which would come installed on its computers. But Jobs saw another challenge: What good was all that music on your hard drive if you could listen to it only when you were at your desk?

Sony had sold something like two hundred million Walkmans to people who wanted to listen to cassette tapes and compact discs on the go. When Jobs and his team surveyed the digital music players in the market, well, they didn't have very polite words to describe them. Most couldn't hold more than a CD or two of music and could play for only a couple of hours before the battery died. Music took forever to download.

Jobs was certain his team could do better—and have a product out by Christmas.

He had a head start; Apple already had nifty software

called FireWire that could move large files quickly. Video-camera makers had been using it to transfer video, but it hadn't yet been used for music.

On a trip to Japan, Jon Rubinstein, Apple's senior vice president of hardware, learned that electronics manufacturer Toshiba had developed a tiny disk drive, less than two inches in diameter, that had five gigabytes of memory—enough to store one thousand digital tunes. The engineers weren't sure what to do with it, but Rubinstein knew right away. "I went back to Steve and I said, 'I know how to do this. I've got all the parts.'"

Jobs told him to go for it, and authorized $10 million, enough to buy all of the disk drives that Toshiba could make so that only Apple would have them.

An expert engineer was hired, a team was assembled, and work began on pulling together the software, screen, and computer chips that a music player would need. Initially, Jobs met with the group every two or three weeks, but once proto-types were built, he checked in every day. And every day there were things to fix: It wasn't loud enough for his forty-six-year-old ears. The sharps weren't sharp enough. The menu was too pokey. Or there were too many steps. Jobs insisted on getting to a song in less than three clicks.

The battery was a particular challenge. The more the hard drive had to work, the quicker the battery ran down. In time, the engineers decided to load several songs at a time into the player's memory, which left more juice in the batteries. The iPod came together in a package about the size of a deck of cards, with a battery that could play music for up to ten hours.

Just as he had left the cursor keys off the first Mac and the floppy drive out of the iMac, Jobs had quirky requests. He wanted only FORWARD, BACK, and PAUSE buttons, and the team had to convince him to add a MENU button. But he drew the line on an on-off button. The answer was simply "No." The player would go to sleep by itself if it wasn't in use.

To make the device look substantive rather than disposable, Jony Ive encased it in pure white—an "unmistakable shocking neutral," he called it—with a stainless steel back, and he insisted on the white headphones. Another executive suggested the scroll wheel, which would speed up the scrolling as you go, so that users could easily and quickly navigate hundreds of songs. Over about a week, the wheel and the menus came together. "Once that user interface clicked, it was like, 'Oh my God, this is gonna be so cool,'" Jobs said.

A copywriter suggested the name Pod, as in "Open the pod bay door, Hal," from the movie *2001: A Space Odyssey*. Consistent with the iMac, it became the iPod.

The ad agency sold Jobs on using images of dancing silhouettes. Figuring he could sell more Macs to support the music experience, Jobs moved advertising money to the iPod from the iMac, allowing him to greatly outspend the competition.

Despite Jobs's excitement, the mood for the October 23, 2001, press conference was subdued. The World Trade Center buildings in New York and the Pentagon in Washington had been attacked just a few weeks before and people weren't in the mood to shop or buy. Air travel had been shut down temporarily and had restarted with far more security. Daily business had come to a near halt.

But Jobs pressed on. Building the drama of the debut, he showed front and back images of the new device on a giant screen, and then pulled the white iPod from his jeans. "This amazing little device holds a thousand songs—and fits in my pocket," he said. The audience was impressed—until he got to the $399 price tag, steep for a music player. (One cynic would later suggest the name meant "idiots price our devices.")

The iPod was clearly cool, but it didn't rocket out of the gate like the iMac. It began to gain converts gradually, selling just under a million in the first year and a half, though new models were introduced. One big reason was there still wasn't a great way to get music for it. Napster shut down in 2001 after losing its court battles with the music companies. For the most part, to put music on your iPod, you had to import tunes from your own CDs or get it from another service, probably an illegal one.

The music industry, uncertain about how to stem the free exchange of music, was offering subscriptions to music services, sort of like a custom radio station. You could listen to songs but you couldn't store and keep them.

While Jobs was working on a better solution to the music problem, Apple was also composing a replacement for the colorful iMac. Though six million of the adorable computers were sold, the company was still losing market share to Windows.

Jobs wanted the next computer to take advantage of new flat-panel displays, which were bigger and more vivid than the old rounded ones. As happened with so many other Apple projects, this one had to go back to the drawing board—just as the first *Toy Story* had to be rewritten. The version Ive originally brought him was a more svelte version of the old iMac. "There was nothing wrong with it," Jobs said. "It was fine. Really, it was fine." Except that he didn't love it.

He invited Ive to his Palo Alto home and together they walked through the vegetable garden and apricot grove that Powell had planted after they bought an adjacent lot. Jobs coached Ive on his vision: "Each element has to be true to itself," he said. The old iMac was puffy as a pillow. The new one was to feature a flat screen. So, Jobs asked him, "Why have a flat display if you're going to glom all this stuff on its back? Why stand a computer on its side when it really wants to be horizontal and on the ground?"

The new iMac, Jobs told him, should look be more like flowers in the garden. "It should look like a sunflower."

Not coincidentally, it sort of did. The larger flat screen floated in the air, attached to a movable chrome neck on top of an inverted flower-pot base. After two years of design work, it was rolled out in 2002. But by the time its impact might be felt, something else was going on: The music business was finally taking off.

After the iPod was introduced, Jobs began a campaign to convince the music companies that he could create a business where even young people would once again pay for their music—but this time, one song rather than one album at a time. Given his outsider status, there was immediate opposition, especially to selling songs individually for ninety-nine cents each. (Of course, Apple would get a piece of each sale.) Some opposed it for artistic reasons. Others wanted to keep selling whole albums even though most customers really only wanted to hear a few songs. In reality, however, the horse had long been out of the barn. People were already breaking up albums and making their own mixes.

Before long, it was clear Jobs had something to offer that others didn't. He had the "whole widget," as he liked to call it. Each recording company had only its artists and its albums.

Software companies had only their jukebox programs. But Apple could offer an all-in-one package—easy-to-use jukebox software, an elegant iPod, and a store for downloading whatever tune you wanted to hear that meshed seamlessly with the software.

To keep the downloading process aboveboard, it also offered protections, allowing music lovers to play their songs on multiple computers and iPods registered to them. But they wouldn't be able to e-mail purchases, transfer songs from an iPod to a computer (thus sharing their music collection with a friend), or copy songs from someone else's computer. "It is corrosive to one's character to steal. We want to provide a legal alternative," Jobs told *Rolling Stone.*

Jobs lobbied executive after executive to win them over. He also reached out to artists, from Bono to Sheryl Crow to rapper Dr. Dre. He pleaded with Irving Azoff, manager of the Eagles, to encourage the rock band to allow their music to be sold. One by one, they came on board.

In late April 2003, Jobs unveiled the iTunes store for Mac owners, with about two hundred thousand songs in stock and more to come. Apple had predicted it would sell a million songs in six months. It sold its first million in six days, and no one would ever look back.

In short, the iTunes software/iPod player/iTunes store trio perfectly captured all the things that Apple did best into one cohesive package. "It combines Apple's incredible technology base with Apple's legendary ease of use with Apple's awesome design," Jobs said. "Those three things come together in this, and it's like, *that's what we do.*"

In October, Apple opened the iTunes store for Windows. In announcing the store, Jobs chose to walk onstage to an unusually sentimental song. The country great Johnny Cash had died recently, and Jobs chose one of his songs, an old Beatles song called "In My Life" that Cash recorded not long after his wife died.

Jobs had listened to the song after Cash had died and was moved by it. He chose it, he said, because "to me it's just one of those reminders of how powerful music can be in your life."

With that final step, Apple's first real break from its stand-alone roots, its move into music really took off. By April 2004, it had sold one hundred million songs from the iTunes store—and less than two years later, it celebrated its *billionth* download.

After selling fewer than two million iPods between 2001 and 2003, it would sell more than 10 million by early January 2005. It would introduce a "Mini" and a tiny, inexpensive "Shuffle" that could hold only a hundred songs, and later a "Nano." By mid-2006, just a little more than a year later, total sales of iPods would reach 58 million units.

More significantly, music and iPod sales would now make up about half of Apple's total sales.

And there was more to come. Writing in *Fortune* in 2001, longtime Jobs chronicler Brent Schlender predicted that "you don't have to be a rocket scientist to imagine how Apple might one day build other configurations of the iPod outfitted with, say, a larger full-color screen, or the ability to work with other iApps that manage video clips and personal calendars." Someday, he predicted, the iPod platform might even lead to something like an enhanced cell phone.

Jobs wasn't done by any means. But he had incredible challenges ahead.

Steve's Playlist

As iPods appeared in pockets everywhere, the question "What's on your iPod?" became a way to really understand a person. Reporters asked presidential candidates, potential sweethearts checked out each other's, friends shared their best stuff, and occasionally, even employers asked job candidates.

Music was especially important to Steve Jobs, who was an unabashed fan of Bob Dylan and the Beatles, as well as cellist Yo-Yo Ma. Ma wasn't able to play at Jobs's wedding, but he later stopped at his house and played Bach for him, bringing Jobs to tears.

"You playing is the best argument I've ever heard for the existence of God, because I don't really believe a human alone can do this," Jobs told him.

So what artists were on Steve Jobs's iPod? His biographer, Walter Isaacson, got a peek:

Bob Dylan, represented with fifteen albums and six volumes of bootleg tapes
The Beatles, with songs from seven albums
The Rolling Stones, with songs from six albums
Joan Baez, four albums
Yo-Yo Ma, three albums
Aretha Franklin
Bach's Second Brandenburg Concerto
B. B. King
The Black Eyed Peas
Buddy Holly
Coldplay
Don McLean

Donovan
The Doors
Grateful Dead
Green Day
Janis Joplin
Jefferson Airplane
Jimi Hendrix
John Mayer
Johnny Cash
Joni Mitchell
Moby
The Monkees
Seal
Simon & Garfunkel
Talking Heads
10,000 Maniacs
U2

Part 3

"And one more thing . . ."

Jobs sharing a special moment with Laurene after delivering the keynote address at an Apple developers' conference in June 2011.

19

Cancer

In his 2005 speech to the Stanford graduating class, Jobs promised three stories. The first was about connecting the dots. The second was about love and loss. The third was about death. It was hardly a typical upbeat topic for a graduation speech.

But then Steve Jobs wasn't a typical upbeat speaker.

In conversations with colleagues and occasionally with reporters over the years, he had shared a personal philosophy. "Somebody told me when I was seventeen to live each day as if it were my last, and that one day I'd be right," he told *Fortune* in 1998.

The story made enough of an impression that he repeated it to the Stanford graduates. He remembered it when he met Laurene Powell at Stanford's Business School and backed out of a meeting, and in the many years since his teen years. The prospect of death kept him focused on what was most important to him, he said, prompting him to shift direction when he stopped making the most of each day.

Then the executive who had worked so hard over so many years to keep his personal and family life private shared a most intimate and powerful story. The year before, he said, doctors had found a tumor on his pancreas, and initially thought he might have just three to six months to live. But a biopsy later that day found that it was a very rare kind of pancreatic cancer, one that can be successfully treated with surgery. "I had the surgery and I'm fine now," he said.

It was a poignant story that captured the audience's rapt attention.

But it wasn't quite true.

Call it the Steve Jobs "reality distortion field," or as his wife called it, his "magical thinking."

In the late 1990s, as Jobs was saving Apple and running back and forth to Pixar, sixty miles away, he began to develop kidney stones, which are extremely painful. "I would rush to the hospital and the hospital would give me a shot of Demerol in the butt, and eventually I would pass it," he said.

In October 2003, the urologist who had treated him asked him to undergo a scan of his kidneys, since it had been five years since the last pictures were taken. His kidneys were fine, but the new scan showed something on his pancreas, an organ that sits behind the stomach. In addition to helping with digestion, the pancreas secretes hormones like insulin that help your body regulate blood sugar levels.

His doctor urged him to follow up—but he didn't. A few days later, she called back to tell him, "This is really important."

Jobs, now forty-eight years old, scheduled the follow-up, and as he had told the graduates, the doctors found a tumor. But this was in the fall of 2003, not mid-2004; in fact, it was about the same time that he had chosen the sentimental Johnny Cash melody.

Usually, pancreatic cancer is fast growing and fatal, but Jobs had a rare, slow-growing form called a neuroendocrine tumor, which was in the islands of cells that produce insulin. The doctors recommended surgery, with the hope of catching the cancer before it had spread.

If he had surgery and the cancer had not spread, Jobs's chances of living were very good. Many patients live ten years or more after surgery.

But surgery for this cancer is no small thing. Sometimes it involves removing the tumor and tissue around it. Sometimes, a more aggressive surgery called a "modified Whipple procedure" is required, which involves removing part of the pancreas, the gallbladder, plus some of the stomach, intestines, and bile duct. Essentially, the whole digestive tract is rearranged and rebuilt.

To the horror and shock of his family, his closest friends,

and Apple's top leaders, Jobs decided he didn't want to have the surgery. In his business life, he was often quick with an answer: Something was great or it sucked, it was a yes or a no. But his personal life was rarely so black-and-white. He couldn't decide to be a father to Lisa and he struggled to decide whether to marry. He couldn't even buy a sofa. In the same way, he couldn't come to terms with his need for surgery.

Instead, he redoubled his focus on his vegan diet, avoiding all forms of animal-based foods in favor of carrot and fruit juices. He tried acupuncture, herbal remedies, and other alternative approaches. All his business life, he had gone out of his way to keep customers from tinkering with his products, and he didn't want doctors to tinker with him, either. "I really didn't want them to open up my body," he said later.

Meanwhile, his family and the tiny group of friends who knew about the situation begged him to reconsider. They talked to him regularly. They asked doctors to speak with him. His wife understood his concerns about opening up his body, but tried to convince him that "the body exists to serve the spirit." She recruited everyone she could to change his mind, including his sister Mona Simpson. "It was very traumatic for all of us," one of those in his inner circle told *Fortune* magazine.

In July 2004, he had another scan and the news wasn't good. The tumor appeared to have grown and maybe spread. Finally, Jobs changed his mind, and on July 31, 2004, doctors performed a modified Whipple. From his hospital bed the next day, Jobs sent an e-mail to employees, explaining his rare cancer and saying it could be cured by surgery if caught soon enough. His was, he said, which meant he wouldn't need radiation or chemotherapy. He promised to be back at work in September.

Once again, this wasn't the whole story. During surgery, doctors found the cancer had spread to at least three places on his liver. Did delaying surgery shorten his life? It was impossible to say, since no one knew if the cancer already had spread when it was found nine months earlier.

Jobs began chemotherapy—and that wasn't the only complication. Because of the major surgery, Jobs was told he would need to eat frequent meals and get plenty of proteins, including those from meat, fish, and whole milk products. But as a vegetarian or vegan for most of his life, he had avoided those foods, and he would continue to do so.

Jobs had always been a difficult eater. Over the years, he frequently sent food back in restaurants as inedible, and even as an adult with a family, he would go on binges, eating only carrot salads with lemon, or just apples, or occasionally fasting. His wife, who also had been a vegan, began adding fish and other proteins to family meals in hopes of convincing Jobs to give his body what it needed. But it was an uphill battle.

Using the latest technology available in 2004, doctors

were able to map part of the genetic material in the cancer, allowing them to use very specific, targeted treatments. But the combination of the impact of the surgery, treatments, pain medication, and his diet issues made it difficult for him to put on and keep on weight and at various times, he would look thin and gaunt.

Jobs's health problems created big challenges for Apple. While many top executives would prefer to keep their personal problems private, the choice isn't a simple one when a company's stock is publicly traded. Under securities laws, companies are required to disclose information to investors that could affect the company's future performance, whether it's strong sales of a new product, problems with a current product, or worries about the CEO. After all, investors are making financial decisions based on how the company will do, and they're entitled to have the proper information to make those choices.

Given how vitally engaged Jobs was at Apple and how important he was to products like the fast-selling iPod line and the new iTunes store, his health clearly would have been a concern. But there are no hard and fast rules about what has to be said or when.

Apple never disclosed that Jobs postponed his surgery for months after his diagnosis. That came out only when *Fortune* reported it in a long, critical cover story in 2008. Neither did Apple disclose that the cancer had spread. Instead, the only public information came from Jobs's (untrue) e-mail that his cancer had been caught early and he wouldn't need chemotherapy. Later, when the cancer recurred and he became skeletally thin, he initially claimed he had a hormone imbalance that was affecting his digestion.

A lawyer for the company concluded that Jobs's right to privacy was greater than shareholders' right to know, *Fortune* reported, "as long as he could continue to perform his duties." But other executives have been much more upfront with their investors about their illnesses.

The battle with cancer made Jobs more reflective, at least for a time. In the summer of 2004, just before his surgery, he met with Steven Levy of *Newsweek*. When Levy pulled out an iPod with a microphone to record the interview, Jobs was appalled to see Levy had put a plastic cover on it to avoid dings and scrapes.

"I think the stainless steel looks beautiful when it wears," Jobs said. "I mean, I'm going to be fifty next year, so I'm like a scratched-up iPod myself."

While his thirtieth and fortieth birthdays were celebrated with fancy galas and big-name entertainment, Jobs's fiftieth was celebrated with close friends and family at a surprise party that Powell threw for him at a friend's house.

His brush with death was still very much on his mind when he agreed to speak at the Stanford graduation just a few months later. He told the students that death makes way for the new, and that even they would grow old and be cleared away. "Sorry to be so dramatic, but it is quite true," he said.

Given that, he gave them his most powerful advice:

"Your time is limited, so don't waste it living someone else's life."

Similarly, don't be trapped by what others expect or succumb to their opinions.

"And most important," he added, "have the courage to follow your heart and intuition. They somehow already know what you truly want to become."

Fighting cancer and facing the potential of his own death, Jobs already had decided to follow his heart. With *Forbes* estimating his net worth at more than $3 billion and growing, thanks to Pixar and the iPod, he could have spent at least some of his time thinking about philanthropy and how he might contribute his enormous wealth. But Jobs had never been interested in giving money away. He briefly set up a foundation after he left Apple, but shut it down after about a year.

When he returned to Apple in 1997, he ended all of the company's philanthropy programs, including its offer to match charitable contributions from employees. The programs were never restored while he was in charge.

Jobs rarely participated in fund-raising events or efforts, and said biographer Isaacson, he "tended to be generally dismissive of philanthropic endeavors." He was rumored to have been behind some large anonymous donations, but that was just speculation. In 2010, Bill and Melinda Gates challenged other wealthy families to commit to donating more than half their wealth to charity or other philanthropic causes. Since then, several dozen billionaires and millionaires have made the pledge, but Jobs wasn't one of them.

His wife, Laurene Powell, was a big supporter of education efforts and started an after-school program called College Track to help low-income students attend college. Jobs said her work "really impresses me," but he never visited one of the after-school programs.

Since his illness, a friend told the *New York Times*, "he has been focused on two things—building the team at Apple and his family." The friend added, "That's his legacy. Everything else is a distraction."

Given his health challenges, he could have retired and spent more time with his family while he battled his disease. In fall 2005, his son, Reed, would turn fourteen, Erin would be ten, and Eve, his youngest, was barely school age.

But his first love was Apple and that was his calling. He worked hard to recover from the surgery so that he could get back to the office. Some of his most important work was still ahead.

The executive team behind the iPhone design. From left: Philip Schiller, iPod Boss Tony Fadell, Design Chief Jonathan Ive, Apple CEO Steve Jobs, Scott Forstall, and Eddy Cue.

20

Redemption

Steve Jobs had a long-running issue with buttons and keys.

When he oversaw the first Macintosh, he demanded that the cursor keys be left off so that users would take advantage of the mouse—and he insisted that the mouse have only one button, instead of two or three, to keep it simple. When the iPod was designed, he refused to allow an on-off button and ordered that other buttons be kept to a minimum. In Tokyo, the elevator in the Apple store was button free, stopping on each of the four floors.

The *Wall Street Journal* even suggested once that he preferred mock turtlenecks because there were no buttons to slow him down.

So when Jobs began thinking about an Apple-made phone, one of his first ideas was to get rid of the buttons and take advantage of the power of touch.

The idea didn't come to him all at once, but evolved over time. When he returned to Apple in the late 1990s, he was especially critical of the handheld Newton device, which used a fake pen, called a stylus, for writing on the screen. Jobs thought that was a silly and unnecessary tool. "God gave us ten styluses," he said, wiggling his fingers. "Let's not invent another."

Aware that Microsoft was working on a tablet that used a stylus, he asked his designers if they could come up with a tablet that used touch and didn't have a physical keyboard. The group was already working on expanding how fingers could pinch and swipe to control the track pad on a new laptop, the MacBook Pro, and was studying whether they could translate that ability to use fingers on a screen. In time, the designers did, creating what they called "multi-touch," allowing the forefinger and thumb to open up or pinch in to make the image on the screen to zoom in or out.

When Jobs saw the technology, "I thought, 'My God, we can build a phone out of this,'" he said. So he shelved the tablet project for the time being to focus on a phone.

Why a phone? Not long after the iPod was introduced, Jobs realized that more and more functions were going to end up on cell phones. People didn't have enough hands or pockets to keep track of all their gadgets. Business people might have a cell phone for calls, a Blackberry for e-mail, or a

Palm handheld to keep track of their calendars and address books, in addition to an iPod for music. It was an overwhelming amount of hardware—and he figured that someday it would (or at least should) exist all in a single package.

At the time, however, phones—like the pre-iPod music players—were way too clunky and complex, with tiny plastic keyboards. The touch screen could show a keyboard when it was needed and then hide it when the user wanted to surf the Web or look up a map. "Everybody hates their phone and that's not a good thing," Jobs said. "There's an opportunity there." That was particularly true for a company like his, which made BMW-like products for consumers who were willing to pay up.

In 2004, wanting to get Apple into the game, he called Motorola, which made a popular phone called the RAZR. He proposed working together on a phone that added iPod features. The result was the Motorola ROKR, which Jobs introduced in 2005.

Apple never had been very good at playing with others, and this product was no exception. It was ugly and awkward to use, rather than sleek and slim, and disappointingly limited. It held one hundred songs and no more. In short, it was a flop. Jobs knew his team would have to get cracking on its own design.

Behind the scenes, Jobs began working with wireless

phone companies on an exclusive deal to sell whatever Apple invented. No one knew whether a small but powerful operating system could be created to give the phone computer-like abilities. But Jobs decided, "We're going to do it. Let's try." Just as he and the iPod team set out to make a music player for themselves, he said, "Let's make a great phone that we fall in love with."

While Apple worked on the phone in secrecy, Jobs also had a big, public challenge on his hands. He needed to save Woody and Buzz from corporate bullying.

After the success of the first *Toy Story* and the Pixar public offering, Jobs had been able to negotiate a new deal with Disney that called for Disney and Pixar to split the profits equally from Pixar's next several films. But Disney still owned the rights to the characters.

Pixar had scored more blockbuster hits with *Monsters, Inc.* and *Finding Nemo,* and with two films still to go in the deal with Disney, Jobs tried to cut yet another better deal. But in early 2004, he broke off talks with Disney out of frustration with its management. He threatened to take Pixar's business elsewhere.

In retaliation, then-Disney CEO Michael Eisner soon started to develop Disney sequels to *Monsters, Inc., Finding Nemo,* and even *Toy Story.* The big movie company was about to have its way with Woody and Buzz.

John Lasseter, the creative genius behind Pixar, was beside himself over what Disney might do. When he told Pixar's staff about the split, he started crying. "I was worried about my children, what they would do with the characters we'd created," he said. "It was like a dagger to my heart."

Luckily, the good guys prevailed. In 2005, Eisner was ousted and his successor, Robert Iger, had a different view. While watching a parade at the Hong Kong Disneyland, he was struck by an uncomfortable realization: All of the recent characters in the parade were Pixar's, not Disney's. He and Jobs began to talk.

Though they considered several possibilities, ultimately Disney agreed to buy Pixar for $7.4 billion in 2006. Lasseter became Disney's chief creative officer, and Ed Catmull, the Pixar cofounder who had been running the business day to day, became president of Walt Disney Animation Studios. A *Toy Story 3* would be made, but they would tell the story themselves, the way they wanted it told.

Jobs, who owned about half of Pixar, became Disney's largest single shareholder, with 7 percent of the stock, worth more than $3 billion, and he joined the board of directors. Though some speculated that he might try to run Disney, his attention remained focused on Apple—and bringing out new products like the iPhone.

Pulling the complicated new product together was

tougher than expected. By fall 2006, just a few months before the iPhone was to be announced at the Macworld convention, it still wasn't working. Calls dropped, applications
didn't work, and the battery wouldn't fully charge. "We don't
have a product yet," Jobs told the team coldly, sending them
back to work furiously to get it right.

Late in the game, Jobs made a couple of design changes.
He decided that the elegant screen had to be glass, not plastic, since plastic was too likely to scratch. Glass could scratch,
too, and it breaks, so Jobs had to find a material that was unusually strong. His search led him to Corning Incorporated,
a longtime innovator in glass that had invented Pyrex and
Corning Ware baking dishes. In 1962, Corning developed
"muscled" glass that was used in cars and planes, but it was
discontinued in the early 1990s.

When Jobs heard about the material, he asked for everything Corning could make in the next six months. That
seemed impossible, since nothing was being made at all. But
Jobs insisted. "Get your mind around it. You can do it," Jobs
told Wendell Weeks, Corning's chief executive.

Within six months, Corning had dusted off its old formula,
improved on it, and started up production at a Kentucky factory. The new material, named "Gorilla Glass," covered the
iPhone and eventually hundreds of other consumer gadgets
with a remarkably tough glass.

Even after resolving the glass issue, Jobs was still tinkering. One Monday morning, he walked in and told the designers, "I just don't love this. I can't convince myself to fall in love with this."

Instead of setting the glass screen in an aluminum case, he wanted the glass display to extend further toward the edge of the phone. The designers had to redo everything—the antenna and circuitry—to change the way the whole package looked. It had to be just right.

Under the deal Jobs had negotiated with Cingular, which became part of AT&T, phone company executives didn't even see the phone until a few weeks before the launch. Jobs even convinced AT&T to make the process of signing up for the phone easier. In exchange for exclusive rights to sell the phone, Apple would even get a cut of the monthly fee customers paid for cellular service. But while other phone makers put the cellular company's name on the phone, Apple refused to tarnish its iPhone with AT&T's name.

At the January Macworld event, Jobs touted the iPhone as a "revolutionary product," combining the best iPod ever, a great cell phone, and for the first time, "the Internet in your pocket."

And there was another thing: Apple was dropping Computer from its name. Apple Inc. was a better description of America's foremost consumer electronics company.

Jobs's turnaround was nearly complete—and he had proven without a doubt that his role in creating the personal computer industry with the Apple II and the Macintosh was no fluke. With vision, genius, and grit, he had taken over an Apple on the verge of failure and saved it with a clever and colorful iMac. For several years, Apple could hardly hold on to the markets it had created, shrinking from $7 billion in sales to a low of $5.4 billion for the fiscal year ending in September 2001, just before the iPod was rolled out.

Then, in addition to reviving the personal computer industry and helping create a whole new genre of heart-warming computer-animated movies, he upended the music business with the iPod and the iTunes store. Between 2001 and the end of fiscal 2006, a few months before the iPhone launch, Apple's sales more than tripled, to $19 billion, and its profits soared, too, to almost $2 billion. Its stock, which hit a low of about $7 in early 2003, was trading at more than $80 in early 2007. Someone who bought one hundred shares for $700 at the low would now have stock worth more than $8,000.

With those results, Jobs was remaking the consumer electronics landscape in new ways. "It is not that he invents technologies, he refines existing ones," wrote *New York Times* reporter John Markoff. Even Jobs said so: "I don't want people to think of this as a computer," he said of the latest creation. "I think of it as reinventing the phone."

Journalist and social commentator Malcolm Gladwell put it another way: Jobs was a "tweaker." He explained, "The visionary starts with a clean sheet of paper, and reimagines the world. The tweaker inherits thing as they are, and has to push and pull them toward some more nearly perfect solution. That is not a lesser task."

Wozniak created the circuitry to make a personal computer, but Jobs tweaked the ideas and pushed and pushed and pushed to turn them into the Macintosh. He didn't invent animated movies, music players, or smart phones, but he revolutionized them with a new approach.

Ironically, he also fought back hard against those who wanted to fiddle with his final products. He opposed expansion slots and replaceable batteries, going so far as to use screws that made his products almost impossible for customers to open. "The greatest tweaker of his generation did not care to be tweaked," Gladwell wrote.

In late June 2007, customers lined up to pay from $499 to $599 for an iPhone, depending on its memory, even though most other smart phones were discounted to $300 or less. In the first three months, Apple sold 1.4 million of them.

Sales picked up steam after Apple cut the top price that fall by $200 to $399 and dropped the cheaper model. As always, Jobs carefully protected his baby. In addition to keeping the phone carefully sealed, Jobs wanted to restrict the software that could be used on the phone. But after an outcry from independent programmers chomping at the bit to write applications for the cool technology, he agreed to open an App Store a year after the phone's debut.

Just as the iTunes store on Windows made iPods more useful, the App Store gave the iPhone another lift. In fiscal 2008, Apple sold more than eleven million phones. Its total sales roared to $37.5 billion and profits jumped to $6 billion.

As Apple turned into a giant, Jobs also struggled with his need to control the message and his products. When he was the underdog, reporters and fans were willing to mostly shrug off his feistiness and sharp tongue. But as a much more powerful player, he began to come off as a big bully in the schoolyard.

In April 2010, an Apple employee accidentally left the next version of an Apple iPhone in a bar. The people who found it sold it to the technology Web site *Gizmodo* for $5,000. *Gizmodo* promptly took it apart and shared all its nifty details with the world.

Jobs called a *Gizmodo* editor himself, saying, "This is Steve. I really want my phone back." Over several exchanges, Jobs was firm but also kept a sense of humor, beginning one call with, "It's YOUR NEW BEST FAVORITE PERSON IN THE WORLD."

Apple got its phone back, but it also complained to the

San Mateo County sheriff's department, which kicked in the doors of the journalist who wrote the story and removed several of his computers. Charges were never pressed against the journalist or the Web site, though many in the media felt like the hardball tactics were over the top. The two men who sold the phone were charged with misappropriating lost property.

Some of Apple's directors warned that the company might look arrogant, but Jobs wasn't buying that. "I'm not worried about that, because we're not arrogant," he said.

Then, after the iPhone 4 debuted in 2010, consumers were upset to learn that a flaw in the design meant that holding the phone a certain way caused calls to cut off. The metal band around the phone had a gap on the lower left corner that, when covered, interfered with the antenna.

When a buyer e-mailed to complain, Jobs, who was in Hawaii at the time, had little sympathy. "Nonissue," he wrote back. "Just avoid holding it that way."

But that didn't satisfy fans who had just paid full price and expected more from Apple, nor did the suggestion that they should buy a case. Jobs took the criticism personally and sulked. But he snapped out of it after someone repeated an accusation that Apple was acting like Microsoft. Eventually, Apple responded that its phones weren't perfect. It promised to fix the problem and provide a free case for users who wanted one.

The issues blew over soon enough and Apple continued to roll up enormous sales. Steve Jobs had hit another home run, and that should have been enough. But there was one more thing.

Stock Scandal

Though Jobs's design sense was spot on, his decisions about his pay put his job in jeopardy in 2006.

The problems started back in early 2000, when Jobs was granted stock options. (They allow executives to buy stock in the future at a fixed price, called the exercise price.) That perk increased in value if Apple's stock went up. But in the following year, Apple's stock went down.

In late summer 2001, Apple's board voted to scrap those options and replace them with new ones that reflected the current lower stock price. Usually, the exercise price is set on the day the options are granted. But when these options were awarded late in the year, Apple executives specifically chose an earlier date, when the stock price was cheaper, increasing Jobs's potential profit.

The practice, known as backdating, isn't illegal by itself—but it is if the date change isn't properly disclosed and accounting adjustments aren't made. Apple did neither.

In 2006, the *Wall Street Journal* published a Pulitzer Prize–winning series about how dozens of companies had backdated stock options, allowing their executives to reap extra profit. None, however, were as prominent as Apple and Steve Jobs.

In addition to accepting backdated options himself, Jobs had recommended favorable dates for option awards for other executives, Apple said. But after a special internal investigation, the company concluded he didn't do anything wrong. He didn't benefit personally because the second round of options were never cashed in and because he didn't understand "the accounting implications."

Jobs publicly apologized to Apple shareholders and employees "for these problems, which happened on my watch," adding, "They are completely out of character for Apple." Apple had to restate its earnings and reduce them by $105 million to reflect the backdated options.

The Securities and Exchange Commission didn't take any action against Jobs, but it accused Apple's former chief financial officer and its former general counsel of wrongdoing. Without admitting or denying wrongdoing, both reached settlements with the SEC, paying civil penalties and each giving up more than $1 million in profits from their own options.

21

Life

Steve Jobs could push his teams to develop amazing products and he could whip up a frenzy for their creations. He was able to keep new products so secret that only a couple of dozen people at Apple might know what they looked like. But among all the things he could control, he couldn't control his cancer.

In 2008, his health began to decline as the disease spread into his liver. He was uncomfortable and in pain. In addition, the combination of cancer therapies, strong pain medicine, and his own lifelong food habits made it difficult for him to eat well. He began to lose weight.

Despite his struggle, he continued to lead an innovation machine. Even as Apple was introducing new iPods and iPhones, it was also remaking its Macs with new creations, like the ultra-lightweight and portable MacBook Air,

Opposite page: Steve Jobs, onstage June 6, 2011, at an Apple developers' conference, in what would be his last product announcement.

introduced in early 2008. The personal computer business, which so many people had declared dead a decade before, still was alive and kicking at Apple.

Jobs attributed at least some of the success to the company's intense process of elimination, which meant rejecting far more things than it accepted. "People think focus means saying yes to the thing you've got to focus on," he said. "But that's not what it means at all. It means saying no to the one hundred other good ideas there are. You have to pick carefully."

The work reflected not just his demanding personality and high standards, but also his belief that it was okay to try and to fail. He noted that all artists—including his beloved Bob Dylan—struck out sometimes. In fact, they weren't artists, he said, unless "they keep on risking failure."

Certainly, not all of Apple's ideas worked well. The first Apple television, an effort to corral all the programs, movies, YouTube videos, and home movies you could watch on your television, didn't take off and was scrapped. Another version still hasn't found a large audience, but Jobs, calling the product "a hobby," kept trying.

He drew the line between a swing and a miss, however, and plain old poor performance, and his health didn't keep him from sharing what he thought. In mid-2008, a new e-mail system called MobileMe was supposed to work with both computers and iPhones—but it didn't work well. The system didn't always sync up e-mail properly between devices and some e-mails got lost. Customers were unhappy.

Jobs summoned the team to a meeting and started with a basic question: "Can anyone tell me what MobileMe is supposed to do?"

After he got a good answer, he followed with another question, in strong language: "So why the _____ doesn't it do that?" he asked.

No answer was going to be good enough, and he was brutal and harsh in publicly flogging the team. "You've tarnished Apple's reputation," he said. "You should hate each other for having let each other down!" In front of the whole group, he put someone new in charge.

Eventually, the service was fixed.

Even as Jobs faced his own mortality, he didn't mellow or become more reflective, not at the office or with his family. While he had to know his time was limited, he never could step away from his work.

He went to Hawaii with his family in spring 2008, but even then, he agreed to an interview with *Fortune* reporter Betsy Morris while he was there. When they were done, he asked Morris to turn off her recorder. Then he made a painful confession: "I love my family. And I come here every year. I want to be here," he said. "But it's hard for me. I'm always, *always* thinking about Apple."

Just as when he was young, there was so much that he wanted to do. But his condition was deteriorating. He lost forty pounds in the first half of 2008 on a frame that was already thin, upsetting his family. Worries about his gaunt appearance had reporters and investors speculating about the health of the top executive who didn't just run Apple, but *was* Apple. At first, the company attributed his weight loss to "a common bug." Then, it told reporters and anyone else who asked that Jobs's health was "a private matter."

In truth, as Jobs's form of pancreatic cancer spread, the body essentially began to consume itself, deteriorating and weakening. Jobs's liver was being taken over by the disease. Using the information they had about his tumors' genetic makeup, doctors continued to give him targeted therapy.

That same year, the American banking system faced its worst financial crisis in the last century, toppling some major players. Even as people continued to buy iPods and iPhones, Apple's stock price fell by more than half, to a low of about $85 at the end of 2008, related to both fears about Jobs's health and a deep plunge in the overall stock market.

Late in the year, Jobs cancelled his planned appearance at Macworld along with other commitments, which got tongues wagging again. In a public statement in early January 2009, he blamed his problems on a "hormone imbalance." Finally, later in January, he took a formal medical leave of absence, saying that he had recently "learned that my health-related issues are more complex than I originally thought." The Securities and Exchange Commission opened an inquiry into whether Apple had made honest disclosures. While an individual can keep some information private, deliberately misleading investors is a problem. But the SEC never acted on the issue.

In 2009, Jobs also began to work with former *Time* magazine editor Walter Isaacson on his biography. Jobs first approached Isaacson about writing his life story in 2004, early in his illness. Isaacson, who has written biographies of Albert Einstein, Henry Kissinger, and Ben Franklin, thought Jobs was too young and it was too soon. But they kept talking, and eventually Powell told the writer, "You really ought to do it now." For the first time in decades, Jobs allowed a journalist full access to his work, family life, and reflections.

Jobs's cancer doctor had warned him for months that he might need to consider a liver transplant. Finally, in January 2009, he was placed on a waiting list in California. But the need for organs there was so high that his chance of getting one in time was slim. To hedge his bets, he also went on the waiting list for a transplant in Memphis, Tennessee.

It was a good call. In March, he got a call from Memphis that the liver of a young man killed in a car crash was available. Jobs and Powell flew there immediately, and the surgery went well. But, Isaacson wrote, the doctors found cancer throughout the liver, as well as the membrane surrounding the internal organs.

Given the spreading cancer, the transplant wouldn't be a cure. Cancer cells were almost certainly in other spots in the body. Instead, the transplant primarily bought more time—and was especially tricky because transplant patients must take medicines that suppress the infection-fighting immune system, which could allow the cancer to continue to spread more easily.

Replacing a liver is a long and complicated surgery, and recovery was slow. Jobs had to get up and start walking again, initially holding on to a chair. Every day, his sister Mona Simpson said, he "would get up on legs that seemed too thin to bear him, arms pitched to the chair back," pushing the chair toward the nursing station. There, he would sit in it and rest before heading back.

Powell urged him on. "You can do this, Steve," she said. Each day, he tried to go a little farther.

He got better and returned home at the end of May. In early June, Jobs began having meetings at his home and by the end of the month, he returned to the office, starting his first day right where he had left off—with a string of tantrums.

Back again, Jobs had a chance to add another dent to the universe. The new liver hardly changed his behavior at all. He still sent food back as inedible and humiliated people in public. When one of his longtime trusted colleagues would pull him aside and try to remind him to be gentler, he would say he was sorry, that he got it. Then it would happen again. "It's simply who I am," he said.

"Like many great men whose gifts are extraordinary, he's not extraordinary in every realm," Laurene Powell told Isaacson. "He doesn't have social graces, such as putting himself in other people's shoes, but he cares deeply about empowering humankind, the advancement of humankind, and putting the right tools in their hands."

In November 2009, *Fortune* named him "CEO of the Decade," saying, "the past decade in business belongs to Jobs." Calling him "a showman, a born salesman, a magician who creates a famed reality-distortion field, [and] a tyrannical perfectionist," the magazine noted that in ten years, "he has radically and lucratively reordered three markets—music, movies, and mobile telephones—and his impact on his original industry, computing, has only grown." No wonder, it said, he was a worldwide celebrity.

He also had one more product up his sleeve. With iPhone sales soaring, it was time to bring that tablet idea off the shelf. Working with Jony Ive, Jobs settled on a rounded rectangle, light enough and inviting enough to pick up with one hand, big enough to read a book on, yet small enough to be easy to throw into a bag or briefcase.

In January 2010, still looking thin, he returned to the stage to introduce the iPad, a touch-driven tablet with prices from $499 to $829. The usual enthusiastic response to a new Apple product was muted. Without a keyboard, the tablet didn't really replace a computer. It did many of the same cool things that an iPhone did, but it didn't fit in your pocket. Some reviewers and even prospective customers had a hard time seeing what it was for.

Within hours, about eight hundred e-mails poured in to Jobs's account, most whining about what the tablet didn't have. "I kind of got depressed," Jobs admitted. "It knocks you back a bit."

None of the whiners, however, had seen the tablet up close or held it in their hands. After it arrived in April, the tune changed. The tablet might not have had a lot of clear uses right away, but it was a marvel to hold and play with. In developing the iPod, iPhone, and now the iPad, the writer Stephen Fry noted, Jobs, Ive, and the Apple team understood and figured out how to capture the intensely personal relationship that can develop with the things we hold and handle every day. As Ive told him: "For us, it is all about refining and refining until it seems like there's nothing between the user and the content they are interacting with."

In the same way the iPod changed the business of buying music, Jobs and the iPad created new possibilities for electronic books. The iPad was a music player, game machine, and Internet surfer, but it was also a book reader. Until the iPad came out, Amazon and its Kindle had dominated the business. Now, with another device and the iBookstore, publishers had more say in how their e-books were priced and readers had more choices.

Apple sold 7.5 million iPads between April and the end of September 2010. Altogether, with that new product, the fast-growing iPhone, and revved-up Macs, Apple's sales topped $65 billion in its fiscal 2010 year-end. It had grown 50 percent in one year, and its profits reached $14 billion, or 21 cents of every $1 in sales, roughly three times the profit that the typical company brings in per dollar.

Then, in May 2010, Apple became the most valuable technology company in the world. Based on its stock price, investors valued it at $222 billion, just past Microsoft's $219 billion. While Microsoft's value would pretty much stand still through 2011, Apple's would roar ahead, closing 2011 at $376 billion.

Jobs, however, was focused on other things, the personal goals he had set to push through his illness. He was building an elegant yacht that he hoped to someday travel on with his family. As Dylan had sung, "He not busy being born is busy dying," and Jobs realized that if he didn't keep planning for a future, he wouldn't have one.

He and his son, Reed, adored each other, and he dearly wanted to see Reed graduate from high school. He reveled in the moment when it came in June 2010, e-mailing from the ceremony, "Today is one of my happiest days." At a party that night, Reed danced with every family member, most memorably with his dad.

Jobs's relationship with his daughters was more complicated. Lisa, now in her early thirties, came to visit him twice in Memphis. Then she and her father went through another months-long period without even a phone call. In 2011, she came back to Palo Alto to see him.

His youngest, Eve, on the verge of her teen years, was willful and determined like her dad, and was the one who was most effective at letting him know what she expected.

Erin, in her mid-teens, dearly wanted to go to the Oscars with her father in 2010, but he wouldn't hear anything of it. But Jobs was able to fulfill a promise to take her to Kyoto, Japan. They had planned the trip in 2008, but had to cancel when he was so sick. In 2010, he initially cancelled again, but then came through in July. Like Lisa, Erin had the chance to eat sushi and soba noodles with her dad and visit Zen Buddhist temples, a special bonding experience. She acknowledged to Isaacson that her father wasn't always very attentive, but said that was okay. "I know the work he's doing is very important," she said. "I don't really need more attention."

By late 2010, the cancer reared up again. For a time, Jobs was unable to eat and had to be fed intravenously. He was weak and in increasing pain. His weight fell to 115 pounds, more than fifty pounds below normal. Powell sought out eating disorder specialists and others, but it didn't help.

In January 2011, Jobs took another medical leave of absence to "focus on my health." The next few months were up and down as doctors tried new treatments. He would get better and then relapse. He turned fifty-six in February, and in March, he was eating again and feeling more energetic. He rallied enough to unveil the slightly lighter, more spry iPad 2, with its cool magnetic cover. The crowd cheered when he loped on the stage, giving him a standing ovation. He also managed to appear again on June 6 to introduce Apple's iCloud service, which would allow users to sync and store their music, photos, and other digital possessions in one digital storage and organization center.

One by one, the people he had worked with, tangled with, berated, and loved came by to say their good-byes. Bill Gates came in through the often-unlocked back door and spent three hours reminiscing and talking about technology, education, and their families. He and Jobs agreed they had been fortunate to marry the right women and to have good kids.

But they would never see completely eye to eye. Gates congratulated Jobs on saving Apple and "the incredible stuff" he had created. He admitted that Jobs's all-in-one approach, making the software and hardware, had worked. "Your model worked, too," Jobs said of Microsoft's software-only approach.

Both of them, of course, still believed his own approach was best.

Jobs came close to dying twice over the summer, but rallied back. It happened so many times that it was hard to believe that he wouldn't keep going. In late summer, Isaacson visited Jobs to go through photographs for the book. Too ill to sit up, Jobs was curled up in bed.

They had talked about his work, his likes and dislikes, and about God. Jobs told him he was "fifty-fifty on believing in God." But, he said, "I like to think that something survives after you die."

After reflecting on that, he added, "But, on the other hand, perhaps it's like an on-off switch." That brought a small smile to his face. "Maybe that's why I never liked to put on-off switches on Apple devices," he said.

On that last visit, Isaacson asked him why he had agreed to the book, given how much he valued his privacy. "I wanted my kids to know me," he said. "I wasn't always there for them, and I wanted them to know why and to understand what I did."

Jobs told Isaacson that he didn't plan to read the book for a while, maybe a year. Perhaps succumbing to the reality distortion field, Isaacson left feeling that perhaps Jobs would be around for a while.

On August 24, however, Jobs resigned as chief executive of Apple. He wanted to do it in person, though he needed a wheelchair to attend. Before the directors who had supported him for so long, he read a letter he had composed:

"I have always said if there ever came a day when I could no longer meet my duties and expectations as Apple's CEO, I would be the first to let you know. Unfortunately, that day has come."

He recommended Tim Cook be named CEO, and added, "I believe Apple's brightest and most innovative days are ahead of it. And I look forward to watching and contributing to its success in a new role."

He still planned to work on new products and give marketing advice, as long as he was able to do so.

On October 5, 2011, with his wife, his children, and both of his sisters near, Steve Jobs passed away.

Since he was a young man, he had told people, "Life is short and we're all going to die really soon." It was dramatic, and it was also true. This life, in particular, was way too short.

Shortly after Jobs's death, fans left tributes to him at his family home.

22

Legacy

Though Steve Jobs had battled cancer for years, somehow his death felt unexpected.

Within hours after the news came out, there was an outpouring of grief from around the world that was unprecedented for a business executive. In front of Apple's headquarters at One Infinite Loop in Cupertino, in front of the Jobses' home in Palo Alto, in front of Apple stores from San Francisco to New York to China, people came to pay their respects. They left flowers and candles and hundreds of personal thank-you notes stuck onto the store windows. They left apples, whole and bitten. They brought their iPhones and their iPads, with messages of sadness and appreciation.

It was as if a world-famous movie star or a rock star had died. U2's Bono called Jobs "the hardware software Elvis." His face was on the cover of magazines from *People* to *The*

Economist, and many publications rushed out special issues commemorating his life, which flew off the shelves.

In her eulogy, which was reprinted in the *New York Times,* Mona Simpson shared her brother's loyalty, his love of beauty, his incredible tenacity, and his hard work. Before he lost consciousness for the last time, she wrote, "He'd looked at his sister Patty, then for a long time at his children, then at his life's partner, Laurene, and then over their shoulders past them.

"Steve's final words were:

'OH WOW. OH WOW. OH WOW.'"

Still in his prime years as a businessman, he had left much unfinished. He had been deeply involved in plans for Apple's new headquarters, going through design after design, and insisting that it include the apricot orchards that dotted the valley when he was a boy. He had hoped Apple would figure out a better way to provide television to the masses. And realizing that many kids are no longer assigned lockers, he hoped to find a way to make textbooks more available electronically, perhaps by selling iPads with textbooks already loaded.

He left a company in mid-roar. The Apple he ran was fifteen times bigger than the one he took over in 1997. In the fiscal year that ended just before he died, Apple recorded sales of $108 billion, reflecting even faster growth than the year before. Nearly 24 cents of every $1 of sales was pure profit. Though his computers and smart phones were among the most expensive on the market, Apple had sold more than

72 million phones, more than 42 million iPods, 32 million iPads, and almost 17 million computers in one year.

He had become phenomenally wealthy, worth an estimated $7 billion, according to *Forbes* magazine, with the largest piece from his Disney stock, followed by his Apple holdings.

Only a few business icons in history changed a single industry, but Jobs had remade several. He wasn't the creator of the personal computer, but he was the voice and face of the revolution. He didn't make the wonderful, computer-animated Pixar movies, but he made them happen. He put digital music and the Internet in our pockets in an elegant way, and he made our lives easier by insisting that every gadget Apple made—and thus, the gadgets that many others made in response—be simple and fun to use.

At a memorial service for Apple employees, Tim Cook, Apple's new CEO, said that one of the lessons Jobs taught him was that "simple can be harder than complex. You have to work hard to get your thinking clear enough to make it simple. But it's worth it in the end, because once you get there, you can move mountains."

It would be easy to get hung up on Steve Jobs's quirkiness and to focus on his ugly side—his temper tantrums, his impatience, how cold and uncaring he could be, how ridiculously high his expectations were, and how demanding he was of those around him. Even Simpson noted in her eulogy

266

Apple CEO Tim Cook speaks at the memorial service for Steve Jobs at Apple headquarters.

that he went through sixty-seven nurses before finding three he trusted.

But ultimately, he was like his products. His Macintosh had too little memory and no cursors keys, his iMac was missing a floppy drive, his iPod didn't have on-off switch. Each was brilliant—and also flawed. But you could overlook the very real imperfections because the rest of the package was so amazing. Many executives and engineers stayed at Apple for years, enduring Jobs's endless demands because they did great work under him, maybe better work than they would have done otherwise.

As much as he pushed them, Jobs didn't want the people he worked with to try to guess what he wanted or to try to be him. "Among the last advice he had for me and all of you," Cook said, "was to never ask what he would do. 'Just do what's right,' he said."

More than gadgets, Steve Jobs left the lessons that he spelled out so powerfully in his Stanford speech and in the way he lived:

He trusted that the dots would connect. He believed the reward was in the journey.

He followed his heart. He didn't settle for okay.

He did what he loved. And if he didn't love what he did, if he didn't believe it was great work, he redid it again and again.

He tried to live each day as though it really mattered, even before he had cancer.

Oh, and there was one other thing. In a 1998 interview and again at the Stanford graduation, he recalled *The Whole Earth Catalog,* an unusual publication that was popular when he was in high school. In the final issue, he remembered, the back cover had a photo of a remote country road.

The caption read: "Stay Hungry. Stay Foolish."

And now, he said, "I wish that for you."

Stay
Hungry
Stay
Foolish

Time Line

February 24, 1955
Jobs is born and soon adopted by Paul and Clara Jobs, who name him Steven Paul.

1967
The family moves to Los Altos, California, so that Jobs can attend a better school.

December 1979
Jobs and other Apple staff visit Xerox PARC and discover new computer technologies, including the GUI and the mouse.

1968
Jobs sees the first personal computer, the HP 9100A, which was actually a large desktop calculator.

May 17, 1978
Jobs first child, Lisa Brennan-Jobs, is born.

April 15–17, 1977
Jobs debuts the Apple II at the West Coast Computer Faire in San Francisco.

Approx. 1970
Jobs is introduced to Steve "Woz" Wozniak, future Apple cofounder.

September 1971
Woz calls Jobs to tell him about blue boxes, which can make free long-distance phone calls. Woz makes one, and the two end up selling the boxes.

February 1977
Markkula hires Mike Scott as president of Apple.

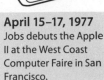

January 1977
Apple Computer moves into its first real offices on Stevens Creek Boulevard in Cupertino, California.

January 3, 1977
Mike Markkula, an investor, supplies $250,000 initial financial backing in exchange for a one-third interest and Wozniak's quitting his job at HP to work at Apple full-time.

September 1972
Jobs enrolls in Reed College in Portland, Oregon.

December 1972
Jobs drops out of Reed College after only one semester.

February 1974
Jobs moves back home and gets a job at Atari.

Summer 1974
Jobs spends several months in India seeking spiritual guidance.

April 1, 1976
Apple Computer is officially founded by Jobs, Wozniak, and Ron Wayne (who dropped out shortly afterward).

Spring 1976
Jobs receives Apple's first order for fifty computers (which became the Apple I) and sets up shop in his parents' home.

March 1975
Homebrew Computer Club is started.

December 12, 1980
Apple Computer goes public and is valued at $1.6 billion, making Jobs worth $218 million.

February 1981
Jobs takes control of the development team for the Macintosh computer.

December 20, 1996
Apple agrees to buy NeXT, returning Jobs to the company as adviser to the chairman.

November 29, 1995
Pixar goes public. Jobs's 80 percent share is briefly worth more than $1.1 billion.

January 19, 1983
The Apple Lisa is announced, but it is less successful than expected.

April 8, 1983
Jobs manages to woo PepsiCo marketing executive John Sculley to become Apple's new CEO.

November 22, 1995
Toy Story, Pixar's first feature film, releases, breaking Thanksgiving weekend box office records.

August 1995
Jobs's second daughter, Erin Siena Jobs, is born.

September 1991
Jobs's son, Reed Paul Jobs, is born.

July 1991
Jobs reaches a deal with Disney to make three Pixar movies, including *Toy Story*.

March 18, 1991
Jobs marries Laurene Powell.

January 24, 1984
Jobs announces the Macintosh computer with a huge product launch, including the groundbreaking "1984" commercial aired during the Super Bowl.

May 31, 1985
Following a showdown with the Apple board and Sculley, Jobs is removed from operational duties, including the combined Mac/Lisa division.

October 12, 1988
Jobs announces the first NeXT computer.

September 17, 1985
Jobs resigns from Apple and founds NeXT, a new computer company. Over several months, he sells all but one share of his Apple stock.

February 7, 1986
Jobs buys Pixar from George Lucas.

November 1986
After the death of his adoptive mother, Clara Jobs, Jobs meets his biological mother, Joanne Schieble Jandali Simpson, and his sister Mona Simpson.

July 9, 1997
Gil Amelio is ousted as Apple CEO. Jobs remains an adviser, but soon forces most of the board to resign.

August 6, 1997
Bill Gates appears on screen at Macworld to say that Microsoft will invest $150 million in Apple.

September 16, 1997
Jobs becomes interim CEO, or iCEO.

Fall 1997
Jobs launches the "Think Different" ad campaign.

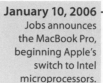

January 10, 2006
Jobs announces the MacBook Pro, beginning Apple's switch to Intel microprocessors.

June 12, 2005
Jobs gives the commencement speech at Stanford University.

January 11, 2005
The iPod Shuffle is announced.

May 6, 1998
Jobs introduces the iMac.

Summer 1998
Jobs's youngest daughter, Eve Jobs, is born.

November 20, 1998
Pixar releases *A Bug's Life.*

November 19, 1999
Pixar releases *Toy Story 2.*

January 5, 2000
Jobs announces the new Mac OS X and officially drops the "interim" from his CEO title.

January 9, 2001
Jobs unveils iTunes.

May 19, 2001
Jobs opens the first Apple Store in Tysons Corner, Virginia.

November 5, 2004
Pixar releases *The Incredibles.*

July 31, 2004
Jobs has surgery for his pancreatic cancer.

October 16, 2003
Jobs opens the iTunes store for Windows.

October 2003
Jobs is diagnosed with pancreatic cancer.

May 30, 2003
Pixar releases *Finding Nemo.*

April 28, 2003
The iTunes store for Mac opens.

January 7, 2002
Jobs introduces the iMac G4 with the first flat screen.

November 2, 2001
Pixar releases *Monsters, Inc.*

October 23, 2001
Jobs announces the iPod, and runs its iconic silhouette commercials.

February 2006
iTunes Store sells its one billionth song.

May 5, 2006
Disney buys Pixar, making Jobs Disney's largest shareholder.

June 9, 2006
Pixar releases *Cars*.

January 9, 2007
Jobs launches the iPhone and drops "Computer" from Apple's name.

June 29, 2007
Pixar releases *Ratatouille*.

August 7, 2007
Apple redesigns the iMac.

January 15, 2008
Jobs announces the MacBook Air.

March 2008
Fortune magazine discloses Jobs's cancer issues.

June 27, 2008
Pixar releases *Wall-E*.

July 11, 2008
The App Store opens.

January 14, 2009
Jobs takes a second medical leave.

March 21, 2009
A liver becomes available and Jobs flies to Tennessee for the organ transplant.

September 9, 2009
Jobs makes his first public appearance following his transplant.

May 29, 2009
Pixar releases *Up*.

January 27, 2010
Jobs announces the iPad.

May 25, 2010
Apple passes Microsoft as the most valuable technology company.

June 24, 2010
Jobs releases the iPhone 4.

June 18, 2010
Pixar releases *Toy Story 3*.

January 17, 2011
Jobs takes another medical leave from Apple.

March 2, 2011
Despite being on leave, Jobs introduces the iPad 2.

June 7, 2011
Jobs shows plans for the new Apple headquarters to the Cupertino City Council.

June 24, 2011
Pixar releases *Cars 2*.

August 24, 2011
Jobs officially resigns as CEO of Apple.

October 5, 2011
Jobs dies.

A picture of the inside of the original Macintosh showing the signatures of all the team members. [Graciously provided by the author's brother, Brad Blumenthal]

Author's Note

In my first business-reporting job in the early 1980s, I wrote about technology and the new personal computer business for the *Dallas Morning News*. I also wrote and edited stories about Apple competitors Compaq and Dell for the *Wall Street Journal*. I never had the chance to see Steve Jobs in action, but certainly followed his career and Apple's ups and downs over nearly three decades.

In early 2011, I had the opportunity to work on a project with Harvard Business School Professor Cynthia Montgomery that included a detailed look at Steve Jobs's management strategy over his career. It was an eye-opening experience, and when this book came along, Professor Montgomery generously granted me permission to use her research notes, which became my launching point.

I am grateful to Terry Anzur and Carlton Ho for filling me in on the Homestead High class of 1972, to Rob Cook, a Pixar retiree, and Dave Culyba of Carnegie Mellon for explaining the math of computer animation, and to *WSJ* colleagues Walt Mossberg, Jim Carlton, and Steve Yoder for taking the time to share their thoughts about Steve Jobs. Thanks also go to Brad Blumenthal and Otis Ginoza for providing photographs.

As always, I am indebted to the hardworking librarians at the Dallas Public Library, especially in Interlibrary Loan, who keep books moving despite deep and endless budget cuts.

"Real artists ship," Steve Jobs said, and I was incredibly fortunate to work with a number of real artists. The insightful and amazing Jean Feiwel conceived this project and trusted me with it, and she and Lauren Burniac were the best of editors, behind me from beginning to end. Jane Liddle backed me up with the world's most efficient copyedit; Katie Cline, Rich Deas, and Ashley Halsey brought their creativity to the design, Anna Roberto, Holly West, and Debbie Cobb pulled the photos together, and Nicole Moulaison and Dave Barrett brought it all together into a real book.

Special thanks go to my agent, Ken Wright, who is the best partner one could ask for in this business. Diana Fenves and the aptly named Ellen McIntosh jumped in to help with research and Ellen compiled a draft of the glossary. Becky Bull made a special trip to the Stanford University archives to read the original Apple prospectus.

Finally, I especially appreciate my family, Scott, Abby, and Jenny, who read drafts, listened, and provided incredible support even when I disappeared for days on end. They are, truly, insanely great.

Bibliography

Because Steve Jobs burst into the public limelight in his early twenties, at the beginning of the computer revolution, and stayed there through his whole life, he has been the subject of an enormous number of books and newspaper and magazine stories. At least ten books chronicle some part of the Apple company story and a handful profile him alone. In addition, Jobs is a player in books written about Pixar and Atari, and in memoirs by John Sculley and Steve Wozniak, among others.

With his good looks, silver tongue, and genuine passion, he was the ultimate cover boy, appearing eight times on the cover of *Time* magazine and at least a dozen times on the cover of *Fortune*. He also appeared on the cover of *Rolling Stone, Inc., Wired, Newsweek,* and what is now called *Bloomberg Businessweek*.

In writing this book, I consulted most of the books available on Apple, Jobs, and his related companies and former colleagues; a large number of cover stories; and many, many other news and feature articles. In addition, I interviewed some former classmates to better understand his school years, found oral histories, tracked down original financial documents for Apple and Pixar, and interviewed key journalists who covered him. A wealth of YouTube videos allowed me to see him speak and unveil some of Apple's most iconic products.

A few sources are worth an extra mention: In the early 1980s, journalist Michael Moritz had access to Jobs, Jobs's family, and friends in reporting a book on Apple's founding— until Moritz contributed some reporting to *Time* magazine. After the story was juiced up by a New York editor and became "The Updated Book of Jobs," Jobs cut Moritz off, but the story and his book, *The Little Kingdom*, are rich with detailed reporting about Jobs's early life. Virtually every book or article about Jobs's early years builds on Moritz's original reporting. A lengthy interview with *Playboy* and a Smithsonian oral history, both available online, fill in many of the remaining pieces of what we know about Jobs's childhood, teen, and college years.

In 2009, Walter Isaacson, a noted biographer and former editor of *Time,* began an authorized biography of Jobs. The two met some forty times over two years, and Isaacson also interviewed dozens of Jobs's friends, family members, and coworkers, giving him extraordinary insight into his subject. His five-hundred-plus-page biography, *Steve Jobs,* is worth reading for ambitious readers who want the most detailed account of this unusual and remarkable life.

Beyond the books, a few journalists covered Jobs for many

years. Brent Schlender, a former *Wall Street Journal* colleague and longtime *Fortune* writer, wrote a number of cover stories with penetrating insight and great anecdotes. Steven Levy of *Newsweek* and *Wired* and Jeff Goodell of *Rolling Stone* also broke new ground in their coverage, as did several *Wall Street Journal* writers, including columnist Walt Mossberg, and reporters Jim Carlton, Pui-Wing Tam, and Nick Wingfield, and *New York Times* writers Steve Lohr and John Markoff.

For those who want a better insight into the early days, an early speech and a lot of early Apple materials are available through the Computer History Museum Web site. And if you want to see how a master made presentations, do what many companies recommend: Watch his product launches on YouTube.

Books and Magazine Articles

Brennan, Chrisann. "Jobs at 17: Nerd, Poet, Romantic." *Rolling Stone,* Oct. 27, 2011: 42.

Butcher, Lee. *Accidental Millionaire: The Rise and Fall of Steve Jobs at Apple Computer.* New York: Paragon House Publishers, 1988.

Carlton, Jim. *Apple: The Inside Story of Intrigue, Egomania, and Business Blunders.* New York: HarperBusiness; 1998.

Cocks, Jay. "The Updated Book of Jobs." *Time,* Jan. 3, 1983.

Cohen, Scott. *ZAP! The Rise and Fall of Atari.* New York: McGraw-Hill Book Company, 1984.

Cringely, Robert X., presenter. *Steve Jobs: The Lost Interview.*

Film directed by Paul Sen, produced by John Gau and Paul Sen, 2011.

Deutschman, Alan. *The Second Coming of Steve Jobs.* New York: Broadway Books, 2000.

Elkind, Peter. "The Trouble with Steve Jobs." *Fortune,* March 5, 2008.

Freiberger, Paul and Michael Swaine. *Fire in the Valley: The Making of the Personal Computer, 2nd edition.* New York: McGraw-Hill, 2000.

Goodell, Jeff. "The Steve Jobs Nobody Knew." *Rolling Stone,* Oct. 27, 2011: 36–45.

Hertzfeld, Andy. *Revolution in the Valley.* Sebastopol, California: O'Reilly Media, Inc., 2005.

Isaacson, Walter. *Steve Jobs.* New York: Simon & Schuster, 2011.

Jobs, Steve. Excerpt of oral history interview with Daniel Morrow. Smithsonian Institution Oral and Video Histories, April 20, 1995, accessed online.

Jobs, Steve. Stanford commencement speech, June 12, 2005. Accessed at http://news.stanford.edu/news/2005/june15/jobs-061505.html.

Kahney, Leander. *Inside Steve's Brain.* New York: Porfolio, 2008.

Kawasaki, Guy. *The Macintosh Way.* Glenview, Ill.: Scott Foresman and Company, 1988, accessed via http://guykawasaki.typepad.com/TheMacintoshWay.pdf.

Levy, Steven. *Insanely Great: The Life and Times of Macintosh, the Computer that Changed Everything.* New York: Penguin Books, 2000.

———. *The Perfect Thing: How the iPod Shuffles Commerce, Culture, and Coolness.* New York: Simon & Schuster, 2006.

Linzmayer, Owen W. *Apple Confidential 2.0: The Definitive History of the World's Most Colorful Company.* San Francisco: No Starch Press, 2008.

Lohr, Steve. "Creating Jobs." *New York Times Magazine,* Jan. 12, 1997.

Markoff, John. *What the Dormouse Said: How the 60s Counterculture Shaped the Personal Computer Industry.* New York: Viking, 2005.

Moritz, Michael. *The Little Kingdom: The Private Story of Apple Computer.* New York: William Morrow and Company, Inc., 1984.

Paik, Karen. *To Infinity and Beyond! The Story of Pixar Animation Studios.* San Francisco: Chronicle Books, 2005.

Price, David A. *The Pixar Touch: The Making of a Company.* New York: Vintage Books, 2009.

Rose, Frank. *West of Eden: The End of Innocence at Apple Computer.* New York: Viking, 1989.

Rosenbaum, Ron. "Steve Jobs and Me." Slate.com, Oct. 7, 2011.

Schlender, Brent. "How Big Can Apple Get?" *Fortune,* Feb. 21, 2005.

———. "Something's Rotten in Cupertino." *Fortune,* March 3, 1997.

———. "The Three Faces of Steve." *Fortune,* Nov. 9, 1998.

Sculley, John, with John A. Byrne. *Odyssey: Pepsi to Apple . . . A Journey of Adventure, Ideas and the Future.* New York: Harper & Row Publishers, 1987.

Sheff, David. "Playboy Interview: Steven Jobs." *Playboy* magazine, Feb. 1, 1985, accessed online.

Simpson, Mona. *A Regular Guy.* New York: Vintage Books, 1996.

Stross, Randall E. *Steve Jobs and the NeXT Big Thing.* New York: Atheneum, 1993.

Wozniak, Steve, with Gina Smith. *iWoz: Computer Geek to Cult Icon.* New York: W. W. Norton & Company, 2006.

Young, Jeffrey S. *Steve Jobs: The Journey is the Reward.* Kindle edition, 1988.

Web Resources

1983 annual meeting, via YouTube.com: http://www.youtube.com/watch?v=lSiQA6KKyJo

1983 Bill Gates on the Macintosh Software Dating Game: http://www.youtube.com/watch?v=NVtxEA7AEHg&feature=fvwrel

Computer History Museum, computerhistory.org

Jobs memorial service at Apple: http://www.thedailybeast.com/articles/2011/10/25/apple-s-steve-jobs-memorial-service-watch-video-of-5-moving-moments.html

Jobs patents, interactive chart, *New York Times:* http://www.nytimes.com/interactive/2011/08/24/technology/steve-jobs-patents.html

LifeSavers ad from Pixar, via YouTube.com: 1990, http://www.youtube.com/watch?v=Fe6FfROGwqk

Listerine ads from Pixar, via YouTube.com: 1991, http://www.youtube.com/watch?NR=1&v=mFjvu3rFysA; 1992, http://www.youtube.com/watch?NR=1&v=lDU5KSMeDAs

Pixar, How we do it: http://www.pixar.com/howwedoit/index.html

Notes

Introduction
Commencement speech, Stanford University, June 12, 2005, accessed at http://news.stanford.edu/news/2005/june15/jobs-061505.html.

Chapter 1: Seeds
Jobs, Commencement speech; Isaacson, *Steve Jobs,* pp. 3–20; Moritz, *The Little Kingdom,* pp. 36–40; Goodell, "The Steve Jobs Nobody Knew," p. 38; Morrow, Smithsonian Oral History excerpt; Sheff, *Playboy* interview; Sculley, *Odyssey,* p. 166; Cocks, "The Updated Book of Jobs."

Chapter 2: Woz
Moritz, *The Little Kingdom,* pp. 54–56; U.S. Census data; Morrow, Smithsonian; Sheff, *Playboy*; Hewlett-Packard interactive time line, www.hp.com; Isaacson, *Steve Jobs*, pp. 14–19, 31; Frieberger and Swaine, *Fire in the Valley,* pp. 11–13. Don Hoeffler, a reporter for the trade publication *Electronic News*, is credited with first using the term "Silicon Valley" in 1971. Young, *Steve Jobs,* Kindle location 1285–1307; "The Hippies," *Time,* July 7, 1967; interviews with Terry Anzur and Carlton Ho; Cringely, *Steve Jobs: The Lost Interview;* Bill

Fernandez, on *The Last Thing*, PBS, aired Nov. 2011; Wozniak, *iWoz*, pp. 54–55, 60–71, 86–91; Isaacson, *Steve Jobs*, pp. 25–27.

Accounts about when Jobs and Wozniak met are inconsistent. Some accounts say Jobs was a sophomore, which means he would have been fourteen or fifteen. But most also say Wozniak had attended college for two years and was then taking a year off when they met. If that was the case, Jobs would have been fifteen years old and a junior, because the two were four years apart in school.

Chapter 3: Phreaks

Wozniak, *iWoz*, pp. 88–118; Moritz, *The Little Kingdom*, pp. 66–79; Isaacson, *Steve Jobs*, pp. 18–19; Sheff, *Playboy*; Carlton Ho interview; the principal's last name was Bryld, if you want to know. "The Vietnam Lotteries," U.S. Selective Service System History and Records, www.sss.gov/lotter1.htm; Ron Rosenbaum, "Steve Jobs and Me," Slate.com, Oct. 7, 2011; Markoff, *What the Dormouse Said*, p. xvii; Chrisann Brennan, "Jobs at 17: Nerd, Poet, Romantic," *Rolling Stone*, Oct. 27, 2011; Jeff Goodell, "The Steve Jobs Nobody Knew," *Rolling Stone*, Oct. 27, 2011.

Chapter 4: College

Moritz, *The Little Kingdom*, pp. 86–101; Isaacson, *Steve Jobs*, pp. 33–55; e-mail from Gay Walker, Special Collections Librarian, Reed College, Oct. 31, 2011; Young, *Steve Jobs*, Kindle location 1647–1900; Markoff, *What the Dormouse Said*, pp. xviii-xvix; Stanford Commencement speech. In his 2005 speech, Jobs says that he dropped out after six months and stayed another eighteen months. However, news articles and books published in the 1980s report that he lasted one semester at Reed and then hung around another year after dropping out. Jay Cocks, "Updated Book of Jobs," *Time*, Jan. 3, 1983; Sheff, *Playboy*; Young, *Steve Jobs*, Kindle location 1947–1953.

A College Reading List
Moritz, *The Little Kingdom*, pp. 89–92.

Chapter 5: Searching
Young, *Steve Jobs*, Kindle location 1947–2200; Moritz, *The Little Kingdom*, pp. 92–101; Isaacson, *Steve Jobs*, pp. 42–55. Jobs told Isaacson that he spent seven months in India, but that seems unlikely. He started at Atari around February 1974 and was in India by summer. Accounts from the 1980s say that he returned in the fall, indicating a trip of a few months. Sheff, *Playboy*; Cohen, *Zap*, pp. 36, 54–57; Wozniak, *iWoz*, pp. 144–148.

Chapter 6: Apple
Wozniak, *iWoz*, pp. 155–177; Freiberger and Swaine, *Fire in the Valley*, pp. 51–53; Frederic Golden, "Big Dimwits and Little Geniuses," *Time*, Jan. 3, 1983; Wozniak, "Homebrew and How the Apple Came to Be," www.atariarchives.org; Moritz, *The Little Kingdom*, pp. 123–142; Isaacson, *Steve Jobs*, pp. 63–67.

Apple vs. Apple
Alex Salkever, "John, Paul, George, Ringo . . . and Steve," *BusinessWeek*, Sept. 30, 2004; Richard B. Schmitt, "Sour Apples: Beatles Sue Computer Firm in Trademark Flap," *Wall Street Journal*, Feb. 22, 1989; "Apple Inc. and The Beatles' Apple Corps Ltd. Enter Into New Agreement," Apple Inc. press release, Feb. 5, 2007.

Chapter 7: Garage

Moritz, *The Little Kingdom,* pp. 142–179; Wozniak, *iWoz,* pp. 176–186; Isaacson, *Steve Jobs,* pp. 67–77; *Interface,* July 1976, accessed via www.applefritter.com; Wozniak, *iWoz,* pp. 177–199; Young, *Steve Jobs,* Kindle location 3535–4046.

Not Yet Ripe

Apple-1 Operation Manual, accessed from the Computer History Museum, www.computerhistory.org.

Chapter 8: Apple II

Moritz, *The Little Kingdom,* pp. 177–178, 198–211, 249; John Markoff, "An 'Unknown' Co-Founder leaves After 20 Years of Glory and Turmoil," *New York Times,* Sept. 1, 1997; Wozniak, *iWoz,* pp. 196–201, 211–220; Jay Yarrow, "Interview with Apple's First CEO Michael Scott," *Business Insider,* May 24, 2011; Isaacson, *Steve Jobs,* pp. 82–91; Apple II brochure, accessed from the Computer History Museum, www.computerhistory.org; Chris Espinosa, "0x22," blog post, March 17, 2011, at http://cdespinosa.posterous.com/0x22; Alex Pang, ed., interview with Chris Espinosa, June 13, 2000, accessed at http://www-sul.stanford.edu/mac/primary/interviews/espinosa/index.html; Ben Rosen, "Memories of Steve," Oct. 24, 2011, www.huffingtonpost.com; Peter Elkind, "The Trouble with Steve Jobs," *Fortune,* March 5, 2008.

Computer Talk

Wozniak, *iWoz,* pp. 168–172, 180–192.

Chapter 9: Rich

Sheff, *Playboy*; Moritz, *The Little Kingdom,* pp. 268–301; Morrow, Smithsonian; Isaacson, *Steve Jobs,* pp. 92–101; Alex Pang, interview with Dean Hovey, June 22,2000, accessed at http://www .sul.stanford.edu/mac/primary/interviews/hovey/trans.html; Grady Booch, Oral History of Andy Hertzfeld and Bill Atkinson, June 8, 2004, Computer History Museum; Young, *Steve Jobs,* Kindle location 4865–5942; Linzmayer, *Apple Confidential,* pp. 41–43, 59–61; Wozniak, *iWoz,* pp. 222–233, 148–49; Prospectus, Apple Computer, Inc., Dec. 16, 1980; Tom Zito, "The Bang Behind the Bucks," *Newsweek Access*, Fall 1984.

Chapter 10: Pirates

Jobs, Stanford commencement speech; Young, *Steve Jobs,* Kindle location 5647–5653, 6880–6885; Levy, *Insanely Great,* pp. 158–59; Isaacson, *Steve Jobs,* p. 112, 131–132, 142–145, 177–79; Hertzfeld, *Revolution in the Valley,* pp. 19, 24–25, 29–30, 46, 166–67; Linzmayer, *Apple Confidential,* p. 92, 112; Steven Levy, "The Revolution According to Steve Jobs," *Wired.com,* Nov. 29, 2011; Moritz; *Little Kingdom,* p. 132; Butcher, *Accidental Millionaire,* pp. 151–152; Rose, *West of Eden,* p. 56.

Apples for the Teacher

Young, *Steve Jobs,* Kindle location 4652–4657, Sheff, *Playboy.*

Chapter 11: Sculley

Sculley, *Odyssey,* pp. 61, 90, 107–108, 130, 155; Isaacson, *Steve Jobs,* pp. 162–210; Isaacson says the agency never tried to sell the advertising time; it just told Apple that it had. Levy, *Insanely Great,* pp. 180–182, 192; Bro Uttal, "Behind the Fall of Steve Jobs,"

Fortune, Aug. 5, 1985, pp. 20–24; Rose, *West of Eden*, pp. 178, 201, 248–253; Sheff, *Playboy*; Patricia A. Bellow, "Apple Computer Co-Founder Wozniak Will Leave Firm, Citing Disagreements," *Wall Street Journal*, Feb. 7, 1985; Gary Wolf, "The World According to Woz," *Wired*, June 2009; Patricia A. Bellew, "Apple Computer Attempts to Deal with Unrest Caused by Defections and New-Product Problems," *Wall Street Journal*, March 1, 1985; Associated Press, "No job for Jobs Apple chief," *Chicago Sun-Times*, July 26, 1985; Carolyn Friday, "Showdown in Silicon Valley," *Newsweek*, Sept. 29, 1985.

Heroes
Michael Krantz, "Apple and Pixar: Steve's Two Jobs," *Time*, Oct. 18, 1999; Sculley, *Odyssey*, pp. 162, 285; Sheff, *Playboy*; Kahney, *Inside Steve's Brain*, p. 178.

Chapter 12: Next
Jobs Stanford commencement speech; Robert X. Cringely, *Steve Jobs: The Lost Interview*; Isaacson, *Steve Jobs,* pp. 211–225; Michael W. Miller, "Apple's Jobs to Sell 850,000 Shares Valued at More Than $13.5 Million," *Wall Street Journal*, Aug. 2, 1985; Patricia Ballew Gray and Michael W. Miller, "Apple Chairman Jobs Resigns, Citing Firm's 'Hostile' Response to New Venture," *Wall Street Journal*, Sept. 18, 1985; Linzmayer, *Apple Confidential,* pp. 207–213; Joe Nocera, "The Second Coming of Steve Jobs," in *Good Guys & Bad Guys*; Katherine M. Hafner and Richard Brandt, "Steve Jobs: Can He Do It Again?" *BusinessWeek*, Oct. 24, 1988; Phil Patton, "Steve Jobs: Out for Revenge," *New York Times Magazine,* Aug. 6, 1989; Andrew Pollack, "Can Steve Jobs Do It Again?" *New York Times*, Nov. 8, 1987; Alan Deutschman, "Steve

Jobs' Next Big Gamble," *Fortune,* Feb. 8, 1993; Stross, *Steve Jobs,* pp. 3, 233, 291; Deutschman, *Second Coming,* pp. 119–123, 142–143, 156–57; G. Pascal Zachary and Ken Yamada, "What's Next? Steve Jobs's Vision, So on Target at Apple, Now Is Falling Short," *Wall Street Journal,* May 25, 1993; Price, *Pixar Touch,* pp. 93–101, 114–116; Ken Siegmann, "Pixar Can't Seem to Animate Itself," *San Francisco Chronicle,* March 29, 1991.

Thank NeXT for the World Wide Web
Paul Andrews, "Scientist's Modest Proposal Spins into World Wide Web," *Seattle Times,* June 7, 1998; Joshua Quittner, "Network Designer Tim Berners-Lee," *Time,* March 29, 1999; Charles Arthur, "Berners-Lee says Jobs made computing 'usable rather than infuriating,'" blog item, Guardian.co.uk, Oct. 16, 2011; Sir Timothy Berners-Lee, "Longer bio," personal Web site, http://www.w3.org/People/Berners-Lee/Longer.html.

Chapter 13: Family
Isaacson, *Steve Jobs,* pp. 250–283, 294, 556; Levy, *Insanely Great,* p. 143; Rose, *West of Eden,* p. 64; Deutschman, *Second Coming,* pp. 21, 72–74, 138–41, 157–60; "Quotations from Chairman Jobs," *BusinessWeek,* Nov. 26, 1984, p. 155; Steve Lohr, "Creating Jobs," *New York Times Magazine,* Jan. 12, 1997; Cocks, "Updated Book of Jobs"; Lisa Brennan-Jobs, all posted on lisabrennanjobs.net; "Tuscan Holiday," *Vogue,* February 2008; "Driving Jane," *The Harvard Advocate,* Spring 1999, and "Confessions of a Lapsed Vegetarian," *The Southwest Review,* 2008; James Daly, "Counterculture Hero: Steve Jobs," *Computerworld,* June 22, 1992; Stross, *Steve Jobs,* p. 281–282; Gary Wolf, "Steve Jobs: The Next Insanely Great Thing," *Wired,* February 1996.

Woodside

Isaacson, *Steve Jobs,* pp. 275–278; Patricia Leigh Brown, "In Silicon Valley, Tear-Down Interrupted," *The New York Times,* July 15, 2004; Patricia Leigh Brown, "Free to a Good Home: A Captain of Industry's Rejected Mansion," *The New York Times,* Jan. 2, 2005; Henry K. Lee, "Steve Jobs's historic Woodside mansion is torn down," SFGate.com, Feb. 15, 2011.

Chapter 14: Siliwood

Price, *Pixar Touch,* pp. 130–132, 143–156; Deutschman, *Second Coming,* pp. 176–184; Alan Deutschman, "Steve Jobs' Next Big Gamble," *Fortune,* Feb. 8, 1993; G. Pascal Zachary and Ken Yamada, "What's Next? Steve Jobs's Vision, So on Target at Apple, Now is Falling Short," *Wall Street Journal,* May 25, 1993; David A. Kaplan, "High tech in toon town," *Newsweek,* Dec. 4, 1995; Brent Schlender, "Steve Jobs' Amazing Movie Adventure," *Fortune,* Sept. 15, 1995; Burr Snider, "The Toy Story Story," *Wired,* December 1995; Brent Schlender, "Steve and Me," *Fortune,* Nov. 7, 2011; Prospectus, Pixar Animation Studios, Nov. 29, 1995, pp. 21, 54; Thomas R. King, "With 'Toy Story,' Disney Banks on a Computer, Unnamed Stars," *Wall Street Journal,* Oct. 20, 1995; *Toy Story* revenue from www.boxofficemojo.com; G. Christian Hill, "Disney's 'Toy Story' Places Pixar Owner Back on the Saddle," *Wall Street Journal,* Nov. 30, 1995; Schlender, "Something's Rotten in Cupertino," *Fortune,* March 3, 1997; Gary Wolf, "Steve Jobs: The Next Insanely Great Thing," *Wired,* February 1996.

Jungle Cruise

Brent Schlender, "Pixar's Magic Man," *Fortune,* May 17, 2006; Price, *Pixar Touch,* p. 6.

What's Geometry Got to Do with It?

Interview with Rob Cook, retired Pixar vice president, Dec. 19, 2011; "Math in the Movies," Discoveries and Breakthroughs Inside Science, www.aip.org/dbis; "An Interview with Tony DeRose," Mathematical Association of America, www.maa.org, Oct. 15, 2009; Interview with Dave Culyba, senior research programmer, Carnegie Mellon University, Dec. 8, 2011; Karen Paik, *To Infinity and Beyond! The Story of Pixar Animation Studios*, pp. 15, 139.

Chapter 15: Return

Jobs Stanford commencement speech; Steve Lohr, "Creating Jobs," *New York Times Magazine*, Jan. 12, 1997; Lee Gomes, "Apple's Next Step is a Software Gamble," *Wall Street Journal*, Dec. 23, 1996; Brent Schlender, "Something's Rotten in Cupertino," *Fortune*, March 3, 1997; Carlton, *Apple*, pp. 414–430; Isaacson, *Steve Jobs*, pp. 295–321; Cathy Booth, "Steve's Job: Restart Apple," *Time*, Aug. 18, 1997; Peter Burrows and Ronald Grover, "Steve Jobs's Magic Kingdom," *BusinessWeek*, Jan. 26, 2006; Schlender, "The Three Faces of Steve," *Fortune*, Nov. 9, 1998.

Steve's Uniform

Isaacson, *Steve Jobs*, pp. 361–62; Josh Quittner, "Apple's New Core," *Time*, Jan. 14, 2002.

Chapter 16: Different

Deutschman, *Second Coming*, pp. 50–57; Interview with Walt Mossberg, Oct. 28, 2011; Linzmayer, *Apple Confidential*, p. 209; Goodell, *Rolling Stone*, 1994; Lohr, "Creating Jobs," *New York Times*

Magazine, Jan. 12, 1997; Cathy Booth, "Steve's Job: Restart Apple," *Time*, Aug. 18, 1997; Michael Krantz, "If You Can't Beat 'Em," *Time*, Aug. 18, 1997; Isaacson, *Steve Jobs*, pp. 324–338; Nick Bilton, "Steve Jobs, Circa 1997, Reintroducing Apple," *New York Times* Bits blog, Aug. 27, 2010; Leander Kahney, "Interview: The Man Who Named the iMac and Wrote Think Different," CultofMac.com, Nov. 3, 2009; Yumiko Ono, "Some Times Ad Agencies Mangle English Deliberately," *Wall Street Journal*, Nov. 4, 1997.

Steve and Bill Onstage
Transcript, "Bill Gates and Steve Jobs at D5," AllThingsD.com.

Chapter 17: Turnaround
Brent Schlender, "The Three Faces of Steve," *Fortune*, Nov. 9, 1998; Isaacson, *Steve Jobs*, pp. 333–34, 348–357, 364–367, 368–377; Steve Jobs, "Apple's One Dollar-A-Year Man," "Steve Jobs's Magic Kingdom," *BusinessWeek*, Jan. 26, 2006; Michael Krantz, "Apple and Pixar: Steve's Two Jobs," *Time*, Oct. 18, 1999; Lev Grossman, "How Apple Does It," *Time*, Oct. 16, 2005; Anne Vandermey, "Stevie Wonder By the Numbers," *Fortune: The Legacy of Steve Jobs, 1955–2011*, p. 108; John Markoff, "Apple to Post Quarter Profit of $45 million," *Fortune*, Jan. 24, 2000; Peter Burrows and Ronald Grover, *New York Times*, Jan. 7, 1998; Jim Carlton, "Apple Gives Bold Answer to Sub-$1,000 Market," *Wall Street Journal*, May 7, 1998; Linzmayer, *Apple Confidential*, pp. 295–298; Steven Levy, "The Revolution According to Steve Jobs," *Wired*, Dec. 2011; Brent Schlender, "Steve Jobs: The Graying Prince of a Shrinking Kingdom," *Fortune*, May 14, 2001; movie results from www.boxofficemojo.com; Schlender, "Steve Jobs'

Apple Gets Way Cooler," *Fortune,* Jan. 24, 2000; Peter Elkind, "The Trouble with Steve," *Fortune,* March 5, 2008; Geoffrey Colvin, "The Great CEO Pay Heist," *Fortune,* June 25, 2001; Pui-Wing Tam, "Apple Reports First Loss in 3 Years," *Wall Street Journal,* Jan. 18, 2001; "Apple Moves to Scrap Power Mac G4 Cube After Weak Demand," *Wall Street Journal,* July 5, 2001; Jerry Useem, "Apple: America's best retailer," *Fortune*, March 8, 2007.

Packaging

Isaacson, *Steve Jobs*, pp. 78, 347: Leander Kahney, "Steve Jobs Awarded Patent for iPhone Packaging," CultofMac.com, July 22, 2009; Pete Mortensen, "Meet the Apple Pack Rats," Wired.com, Sept. 15, 2005; Miguel Helft and Shan Carter, "A Chief Executive's Attention to Detail, Noted in 313 Patents," *New York Times*, Aug. 25, 2011; Levy, *The Perfect Thing,* pp. 79–80.

Chapter 18: Music

Brent Schlender, "How Big Can Apple Get?" *Fortune,* Feb. 21, 2005; Levy, *The Perfect Thing,* pp. 8–11, 21–22, 53, 77–79, 87–118, 197; Kahney, *Inside Steve's Brain*, pp. 186–88; Isaacson, *Steve Jobs*, pp. 382–410, 445–46; Leander Kahney, "Inside Look at Birth of the iPod," July 21, 2004, and "Straight Dope on the iPod's Birth," Oct. 17, 2006, both Wired.com; Rob Walker, "The Guts of a New Machine," *New York Times,* Nov. 30, 2003; Josh Quittner, "Apple's New Core," *Time,* Jan. 14, 2002; Jeff Goodell, "Steve Jobs: *Rolling Stone*'s 2003 Interview," *Rollingstone.com;* Pui-Wing Tam, Bruce Orwall, and Anna Wilde Mathews, "Going Hollywood: As Apple Stalls, Steve Jobs Looks to Digital Entertainment," *Wall Street Journal*, April 25, 2003; Steven Levy, "The

Revolution According to Steve Jobs," *Wired,* Dec. 2011; Schlender, "Apple's 21st Century Walkman," *Fortune,* Nov. 12, 2001.

Steve's Playlist
Isaacson, *Steve Jobs*, pp. 411–415.

Chapter 19: Cancer
Stanford commencement speech; Brent Schlender, "The Three Faces of Steve," *Fortune,* Nov. 9, 1998; Isaacson, *Steve Jobs*, pp. 452–460, 476–477, 543; Peter Elkind, "The Trouble with Steve Jobs," *Fortune,* March 5, 2008; Sharon Begley, "A Medical Gamble," *Newsweek Special Commemorative Issue: Steve Jobs, 1955–2011,* pp. 28–31; Levy, *The Perfect Thing,* p. 71; *Forbes* 400 ranking 2005, via Forbes.com.

Chapter 20: Redemption
Nick Wingfield, "Hide the Button: Steve Jobs Has His Finger on It," *Wall Street Journal,* July 25, 2007; Isaacson, *Steve Jobs*, pp. 308-309, 432-443, 465-470, 518-520; Walt Mossberg and Kara Swisher, "The iPad: Past, Present, and Future," *Wall Street Journal,* June 7, 2010; Lev Grossman, "The Apple of Your Ear," *Time,* Jan. 12, 2007; Steve Jobs, "Macworld San Francisco 2007 Keynote Address," 11 parts, YouTube.com; Amol Sharma, Nick Wingfield, and Li Yuan, "Apple Coup: How Steve Jobs Played Hardball in iPhone Birth," *Wall Street Journal,* Feb. 17, 2007; Betsy Morris, "Steve Jobs Speaks Out," *Fortune,* March 7, 2008; Price, *Pixar Touch,* pp. 232-244; Fred Vogelstein, "The Untold Story: How the iPhone Blew Up the Wireless Industry," *Wired,* Jan. 9, 2008; Steve Lohr, "The Power of Taking the Big Chance,"

New York Times, Oct. 9, 2011; Mossberg interview, Oct. 28, 2011; Apple Computer Inc. annual reports, 1999 and 2003, and Apple Inc. annual report 2007, 2008; John Markoff, "Steve Jobs Walks the Tightrope Again," *New York Times,* Jan. 12, 2007; Malcolm Gladwell, "The Tweaker," *New Yorker,* Nov. 14, 2011, pp. 52-55; Nick Wingfield, "Apple Price Cut on New iPhone Shakes Investors," *Wall Street Journal,* Sept. 6, 2007; Nick Wingfield, "Apple Opens iPhone to Outside Software," Oct. 18, 2007; Brian Lam, "Steve Jobs was always kind to me," blog post, thewirecutter.com, October 5, 2011; David Carr, "A Lost iPhone Shows Apple's Churlish Side," *New York Times,* May 2, 2010; Nick Bilton, "Two Charged in Missing iPhone Prototype Case," *New York Times* Bits Blog, Aug. 10, 2011; John Boudreau, "Beware of the iPhone 'Death Grip,'" *San Jose Mercury News,* June 26, 2010; Yukari Iwatani Kane and Niraj Sheth, "Apple Knew of iPhone Issue," *Wall Street Journal,* July 16, 2010.

Stock Scandal
Peter Elkind, "The Trouble with Steve Jobs," *Fortune,* March 5, 2008; Nick Wingfield, Steve Stecklow, and Charles Forelle, "Jobs Helped Pick 'Favorable' Dates for Option Grants," *Wall Street Journal,* Dec. 30, 2006; Laurie J. Flynn, "Apple Says Jobs Knew of Options," *New York Times,* Oct. 5, 2006; "High Noon for Heinen," Law Blog, wsj.com, Aug. 14, 2008.

Chapter 21: Life
Isaacson, *Steve Jobs,* pp. 462–63; 476–489, 538–559, 570–71; Betsy Morris, "Steve Jobs, Obsession, and Those Whales," Wired .com, Oct. 7, 2011; Brent Schlender, "The Three Faces of Steve,"

Fortune, Nov. 9, 1998; Adam Lashinsky, "The Decade of Steve," *Fortune,* Nov. 23, 2009; Sharon Begley, "A Medical Gamble," *Newsweek Special Commemorative Issue: Steve Jobs, 1955–2011,* pp. 28–31; Kara Scannell and Yukari Iwatani Kane, "SEC Opens Inquiry into Apple Disclosure on Jobs' Health: Source," Dow Jones News Service, Jan. 21, 2009; Yukari Iwatani Kane, "Apple's Jobs Take Medical Leave," *Wall Street Journal,* Jan. 15, 2009; "Jobs' Biography: Thoughts on Life, Death and Apple," npr.org, Oct. 25, 2011; Stephen Fry, "The iPad Launch: Can Steve Jobs Do It Again?" *Time,* April 1, 2010; Ken Auletta, "Publish or Perish," *New Yorker,* April 26, 2010; Jeffrey A. Trachtenberg, "E-Book Readers Face Sticker Shock," *Wall Street Journal,* Dec. 15, 2011; Apple Inc. annual report, 2011; Yukari Iwatani Kane and Joann S. Lublin, "Apple Chief to Take Leave," *Wall Street Journal,* Jan. 18, 2011; Brent Schlender, "The Three Faces of Steve," *Fortune,* Nov. 9, 1998.

Chapter 22: Legacy

"Bono Calls Steve Jobs 'The Hardware Software Elvis,'" Speakeasy blog, wsj.com, Oct. 7, 2011; Mona Simpson, "A Sister's Eulogy for Steve Jobs," *New York Times,* Oct. 30, 2011; Apple Inc. annual report, 2011; Tim Cook, Apple memorial service, viewed online; Brent Schlender, "The Three Faces of Steve," *Fortune,* Nov. 9, 1998; Jobs Stanford commencement speech.

Glossary

app: Short for application. Apps can be software programs that run on your computer, such as word processors or spreadsheets, or that run on your mobile phone, such as maps and restaurant guides. Apple Macintosh programs have an .APP file to launch them. (Windows programs use .EXE.)

BASIC: A computer language developed in the 1960s to help students learn to write computer programs that can now be used for more advanced programming. It stands for Beginners All-purpose Symbolic Instruction Code.

bit: BInary digiT. The smallest unit of computer data, expressed as 0 or 1.

bozo: A fool or someone who isn't competent. One of Steve Jobs's favorite words to describe people he thought weren't very sharp. A 1960s television series featured a character named Bozo the Clown. Ronald McDonald, who came along a little later, bears a resemblance to the television Bozo.

byte: A storable unit of computer data made up of eight bits. A byte usually represents a single character, such as a number or letter, though some computer languages require two bytes for a character.

central processing unit (CPU): The brains of a computer or the processor, which performs logical and arithmetical operations and executes software commands.

disk drive: A data storage device that reads and writes data to disks.

DOS: Disk operating system. The first operating system for IBM personal computers, written by Microsoft and often called MS-DOS. Using simple commands, it told the computer what to do. Windows has now replaced DOS on PCs. The operating system allows programs to run on the computer.

floppy disk: A type of portable data storage. The first floppy disk measured eight inches diagonally. The next version measured 5.25 inches and was capable of holding three times as much storage. The 3.5-inch disk, which was encased in plastic and no longer floppy, held even more. While an image of a floppy disk is still the icon that you click to save your work on a computer, floppy disks have been replaced by other devices, such as USB flash drives and external hard disk drives, and are rarely used today.

gigabyte (GB): About a billion bytes of computer storage, or 1,024 megabytes.

graphical user interface (GUI): Pronounced "gooey." Using icons, menus, and a mouse as the method of interacting with a computer. The Apple Macintosh introduced in 1984 was the first commercially successful computer to employ a graphical user interface.

hard drive: Also a hard disk drive. A built-in device that stores the programs and files on your computer. A hard disk drive contains round, mirrorlike platters made of glass or aluminum that spin to store and retrieve information.

hardware: The physical parts of a computer system, such as the CPU and disk drives and the computer itself. Monitors, keyboard, speakers, and printers are kinds of hardware often referred to as peripherals.

HTML: HyperText Markup Language. The language of Web pages that allows them to show up correctly on your browser.

HTTP: HyperText Transfer Protocol. The procedure used to transfer data over the World Wide Web.

integrated circuit: Also called a computer chip or microchip, these commonly used chips contain various electronic components, like transistors, resistors, diodes, and capacitors, to make calculations or store data. Microprocessors and memory chips are both integrated circuits.

kilobyte (KB): 1,024 bytes of computer storage.

MAC OS: The Macintosh operating system, pronounced like the letters "O" and "S", which is necessary to make the computer work. The current version in use is Mac OS X, which is pronounced "O S ten."

megabyte (MB): About 1 million bytes of computer storage or 1,024 kilobytes.

microprocessor: Also called a CPU. The brains of the computer, which performs mathematical operations, stores and transfers data, and processes instructions from software and other hardware components. Intel Corporation invented the first microprocessor in 1971.

minicomputer: Typically a stand-alone device about the size of a refrigerator, it was used for business applications that needed more power and memory than a microcomputer, but less than a mainframe computer. Minicomputers have been replaced by networks of small computers linked by a powerful server.

Moore's Law: In 1965, Intel Corporation cofounder Gordon Moore predicted that that the number of transistors on a microprocessor would double every two years, greatly increasing computer power over time. That prediction has basically been true and became known as Moore's Law.

MP3: A popular audio file that is compressed, making it easier to share and download music files.

operating system (OS): The essential program in a computer that maintains disk files, runs applications, and handles devices such as the mouse and printer.

PC: A personal computer. The first personal computer was a kit called the Altair. The term PC is a generic label for computers using the Microsoft Windows operating system. Apple

Macintosh computers are personal computers, but are generally called Macs, a distinction the company has played up with its Mac and PC advertisements.

playlist: An ordered list of songs or videos, such as those played on the radio or on your iPod or other music player.

profit: The amount remaining after all of a company's expenses are subtracted from its revenue or sales. Net income or net profit is the profit remaining after taxes are paid.

Random access memory: Also called RAM. Memory chips that can be quickly accessed. When you open up a program or file, it is loaded into the RAM. **Dynamic RAM (DRAM)** is generally considered the computer's memory and must be constantly refreshed, therefore requiring more power. **Static RAM (SRAM)** chips can retain their contents without being continuously refreshed.

Read-only memory: Also called ROM. Memory chips that hold data permanently and that retain the information whether the computer is on or off. The chip can be written on only once, usually during the manufacturing process.

reality distortion field: The name that engineer Bud Tribble gave to Steve Jobs's ability to convince others to agree to his demands or believe that the impossible was possible. The effect wore off when Jobs wasn't in the room.

revenue or sales: Often used interchangeably, this is the money that a business or organization receives for its goods or services.

semiconductor: Often used to describe the chips or integrated circuits that run electronic products. Also, a material, such as silicon, that can be used to conduct or block electrical current.

software: Computer programs made up of lines of code that tell a computer what to do or allow you to use the computer in different ways.

tablet: A small, lightweight computer designed to go with you. Some tablets use a stylus, or pencil-like device, and others operate by touch.

WYSIWYG: Pronounced Wiz-e-wig, it's an acronym for "what you see is what you get." WYSIWYG means that what you see on the screen is also how it will print out. Older technology required computer users to enter codes to create a document, and then wait to see if it printed out correctly.

Index

Photo Credits